The Expanding World

Towards a Politics of Microspection

The Expanding World

Towards a Politics of Microspection

Michael Cronin

Winchester, UK
Washington, USA

First published by Zero Books, 2012
Zero Books is an imprint of John Hunt Publishing Ltd., Laurel House, Station Approach,
Alresford, Hants, SO24 9JH, UK
office1@o-books.net
www.o-books.com

For distributor details and how to order please visit the 'Ordering' section on our website.

ISBN: 978 1 78099 077 4

A CIP catalogue record for this book is available from the British Library.

Design: Stuart Davies

Printed in the UK by CPI Antony Rowe
Printed in the USA by Offset Paperback Mfrs, Inc

We operate a distinctive and ethical publishing philosophy in all
areas of our business, from our global network of authors to
production and worldwide distribution.

CONTENTS

For Fionnuala

Introduction

In the centuries-old surroundings of Château Beychevelle, an astronomer is asked by a wine connoisseur what he sees in a glass of wine. What he sees, he tells him, is the birth of the universe because he sees the particles formed in the first few seconds. He sees the sun that existed before our own because carbon atoms were formed in that exploding star and he sees the carbon atoms joined up with other atoms to form the physical basis of our earth. He sees the composition of macromolecules which emerged to give birth to life. He sees the first living cells, the development of the plant kingdom, and the cultivation of vines in Mediterranean countries. He sees Bacchanalian orgies and feasts. He sees the selection of the grape varieties, the age-old traditions of the vineyards. He sees the development of modern technology which allows the temperature of fermentation in the vats to be electronically controlled (Morin 1999: 39). What Michel Cassé observes in a glass of red wine is in global terms a *résumé* of cosmic and human history and in local, the specific history of Bordeaux wines. The whole is captured in the part and the part opens on to the whole. A glass becomes a looking glass and whole worlds are reflected in a goblet of fermented grape juice.

The Expanding World is fundamentally about looking more closely at what is around us and acting on that knowledge. It is about considering what it means to have whole worlds reflected in the looking glass of local inquiry. In this extended essay, the intention is to advance what we might call a *politics of microspection*. By this, we mean a form of engagement with the world which is based on an in-depth analysis and understanding (*specere*: to look at) of the local (*mikros*: little). The purpose is twofold. Firstly, the aim is to counter a prevailing culture of disenchantment and particular understandings of globalization

I

by highlighting the inexhaustible variety and richness of the planet. Secondly, the objective is to suggest the implications for politics and society of the development of a way of seeing and doing which is bound up with the local and the proximate.

Chapter One begins by asking the question: Is our world really shrinking? Time-space compression is often held up to be the dominant feature of our age. (Some) people can get anywhere now much faster or communicate with each other instantly. As more space can be covered in less time, the world is said to get smaller and the effects of standardization are felt worldwide. The chapter opposes this view, with a reading of recent developments in mobility, technology and urbanization that argues for the centrality of the micro not the macro; using the example of language difference and translation shows how one can argue that late modernity is characterised not by increasing homogeneity but by growing dissimilarity. By putting forward a notion of 'micro-modernity', the chapter challenges versions of place that see complexity as the sole property of large, metropolitan centres (the 'Modernist' cities of Paris, Berlin, London, New York, Tokyo).

Chapter Two examines the status of humans living in an expanding rather than a shrinking world. Central to the chapter is the notion of the denizen, namely one who lives, or better, dwells knowingly in a particular place. What this might involve is pursued in the areas of tourism, real estate and migration. In this context, the chapter explores the impact of notions of space and time as they define or will define the status of the denizen. Attempts to idealize the local can often lead to misleading and overly positive representations of local community. The chapter argues, on the contrary, that conflict is central to the construction and elaboration of communities in local settings. Small may, on occasions, be beautiful, but is rarely, if ever, peaceful.

Chapter Three focuses on the forms of inter-relation that can be imagined in local contexts in globalized societies and economies. The chapter explores the limits to particular versions of community and suggests that changes in how otherness is viewed have profound implications for a sense of self and the collective in a global age. How the notion of extended time impacts on both the self and the collective is considered in the chapter with a view to embedding short-term predicaments in long-term scenarios.

Chapter Four seeks to address in more programmatic terms the issues raised in the previous three chapters. The chapter divides a politics of microspection into an analytic and operational component and describes what might be included under both these headings. A major concern of the chapter is to show how specific forms of inquiry and various kinds of political, economic, educational and social practices can give real effect to a politics of microspection. A major contention in the chapter is that any form of action to ensure the sustainability of the planet and the survival of its inhabitants cannot ignore questions of social justice and political freedom. Being green means dealing with the unseen and dealing with the unseen means reaching out not closing in.

Leonard Koren in his attempt to define a feature associated with traditional Japanese aesthetics, *wabi-sabi*, notes how for practitioners of *wabi-sabi* 'greatness' exists in inconspicuous and overlooked details. The 'details' take on the world, 'Within the tea room as within all places wabi-sabi, every single object seems to expand in importance in inverse proportion to its actual size' (Koren 1994: 67). Like the astronomer's wine glass or Proust's *Madeleine* or Joyce's native city on a particular day June in 1904, overlooked minutiae are the portals to an understanding of the world. If part of the revolutionary hope of modernism was that art and politics would come together in a great transformative moment, the moment may not so much be past as not yet have come. Surviving into the next century means that all our resources, political, aesthetic, economic must be mobilised.

Dwelling meaningfully and practicably on a planet whose future is deeply uncertain is a skill we must all urgently acquire. *The Expanding World* suggests where we might begin.

Michael Cronin
Labastide-Esparbaïrenque/Dublin
August 2011.

Chapter One

A Shrinking World?

The tag line for the film is 'If you want to be understood, listen'. The problem for the characters in Alejandro González Iñárritu's *Babel* (2006) is that even when they do listen, they do not always understand. The languages of the world are not mutually intelligible. The version of the Babel story which is gravely intoned in the film's preview is explicit about the link between hubris and incomprehension:

> In the beginning all the Lord's people from all parts of the world spoke one language. Nothing they proposed was impossible for them. But fearing what the spirit of man did accomplish, the Lord said let us go down and confuse their language so that they may not understand one another's speech.

As the rifle shots ring out across the Moroccan desert, the implication is that to speak one language is to be all-powerful, to speak many a manifesto for chaos. But of course, it is the film itself ranging across three continents and seven different languages (English, French, Arabic, Berber, Spanish, Japanese and Japanese Sign Language) which recreates the Babelian project. From behind the lens of the camera it is possible to take in the multiplicity of the world in the single frame of the cinema screen. As the narrative rapidly shifts from Southern California to Morocco to Tokyo, the world unfolds before us as if the Tower of Babel was an in fact an observation post, the cinema itself an Observatory for a humanity brought together for our inspection. It is hardly surprising then when checklists are drawn up to establish the incontrovertible fact of a shrinking world that cinema and in particular the cinema output of Hollywood majors is regularly invoked as a shared element in an emerging global culture (Crane 2002).

Anthony Giddens famously, if not particularly memorably, defined globalisation two decades ago as 'the intensification of worldwide social relations which link distant localities in such a way that local happenings are shaped by events occurring many miles away and vice versa' (1990: 64). The emergence of international institutions (IMF, World Bank, World Trade Organisation (WTO)), the spread of global brands (McDonalds, Starbucks), heightened environmental awareness (Chernobyl, the Brundtland report (1987), UN reports on climate change), worldwide protest movements (Vietnam, anti-globalisation protests) are seen as both causes and symptoms of the 'intensification of world wide social relations.' In a particular mythology of time and space, time-space convergence is said to happen at a national level in the 19th century and the first half of the twentieth century and is facilitated notably through the construction of railways and road networks. Time-space convergence at a global level is said to occur in the second half of the twentieth century, enabled through the exponential growth in air travel and the proliferation of IT and telecommunications networks (Thrift, May & May 2001: 4-15)). As the time taken to travel distances is greatly reduced, it is usual to speak of time-space compression as a central feature of the phenomenon of globalisation, though overly simplistic versions of compression tend to ignore the very different experiences of space and time within the same historical frame and in different geographical locations (27-32). The last two centuries might therefore be termed the era of *macro-modernity* where the emphasis has been on assembling the overarching infrastructures which allow time-space compression to become a reality. So the most commonly invoked paradigm of our age is the planet as 'a shrinking world'.

The collapse of Soviet communism and economic reforms in China further added to the sense of the rise of one System under Market (Fukuyama 1992). From this perspective, not only is the world smaller but, to borrow Thomas Friedman's coinage, the earth is flatter. For Friedman, all the world is conceived of as a level playing field, where all compete, however unequally, for the spoils of free trade (Friedman 2006).

The advent of globalization and globalizing processes is not, of course, always or inevitably, seen as a benign development. From the rise of the anti-globalization movement in the 1990s to the meltdown of financial markets at the end of the first decade of the twenty-first century, globalization has become a synonym for a plethora of ills, financial, ecological, social and political (Klein 2007). One constant is the contention that what globalization entails is an irretrievable loss of innocence, a death sentence for diversity and the spread of what I have called elsewhere 'clonialism', the viral spread of corporate, hegemonic sameness (Cronin 2003: 128). As the world shrinks, so do our possibilities for exploring, preserving and promoting difference. The global villages begin to resemble each other in dispiritingly predictable ways, carbon copy model towns presided over by brand uniformity. Pedestrianized zones offer the same glossy retail experience whatever the continent.

Contemporary experience can, however, be approached in another way and this is through the prism of what might be termed *micro-modernity*. By this we mean that by starting our analysis from the standpoint of the local, the nearby, the proximate, the micro, we can conceive of the local not as a point of arrival, the parachute drop for global forces, but as a point of departure, a opening out rather than a closing down, a way of re-enchanting a world grown weary of the jeremiads of cultural entropists. The world of micro-modernity challenges the orthodoxies of global macro-modernity. As a result of the changes that lie ahead of us it is necessary to look not to compression but to expansion, but to expansion of a radically different kind. Whereas previously, emancipation has been thought of as a going further, faster - Marinetti's Futurist Utopia, Marx's accelerated rates of production unleashing revolutionary energies or Edward Luttwak's Turbo-Capitalism - we must now think of liberation as going deeper, slower. In other words, in advocating this shift of perspective, we wish to suggest that it is possible to develop a new *politics of microspection which* seeks to expand possibilities of the local, not reduce them, and which offers the opportunity to reconfigure positively our social, economic and political experience of the fundamentals of space and time. In arguing for a new approach to the local, we want to move away from a dichotomous standoff between the global and the local which frequently paralyses political and cultural analysis. Ursula K. Heise speaks of the theoretical stalemate that results from this 'conflict between a conceptualization of national identity as either an oppressive, hegemonic discourse or a tool for resistance to global imperialism, and of local identity as either an essentialist myth or a promising site of struggle against both national and global domination' (Heise 2008: 7). Heise, for example, is deeply hostile to the tendency of American environmental thinkers to eulogize unproblematically a local 'sense of place' and ignore the larger webs of connectivity that influence or determine the nature and experience of the local in late modernity. Central to her critique is the concept of deterritorialization, namely, that the 'increasing connectedness of societies around the globe entails the emergence of new forms of culture that are no longer anchored in place' (10). Similarly, John Tomlinson claims that the choice of crops to be cultivated by farmers in the most remote corner of the developing world can be dictated by needs of First World markets in much the same way as these farmers may become dependent on the seeds, fertilisers and pesticides sold by transnational corporations. It is not so much affluence as the relative impact of the various forces of global modernity which can dramatically alter a relationship with a locality:

> [I]t is possible to argue that some populations in the contemporary Third World may, precisely, because of their positioning within the uneven process of globalization, actually have a sharper, more acute experience of deterritorialization than those in the First World. (Tomlinson 1999: 137)

Acid rain, radioactive fallout, global warming, bovine spongiform encephalopathy (Mad Cow disease), severe acute respiratory syndrome (SARS) and swine flu are examples of how various ecological and health risks operating globally can have significant local impacts. Fresh, local-grown agricultural produce had to be destroyed in many parts of Europe as a result of a nuclear accident which happened hundreds of miles away in a nuclear plant in the Ukraine. The prevalence of deterritorialization, the transnational nature of risk scenarios or the importance of what Giddens (1990: 126-27) calls 'disembedding' – the existence of networks beyond the local such as international insurance practices that allow the cup made in China to be manufactured and shipped and eventually reach your breakfast table – do not so much invalidate the local as demand that it be thought about in different ways. In other words, it is not a question of presenting an Arcadian version of local pastoral where disparate groups live in an Eden of non-connectedness but of thinking about the local in terms of hybridity, conflict, migration, social production, cultural construction and transformation. To that extent, microspection in this essay is to be understood as a process rather than a state. The local that is constructed through the process of microspection, is, in a sense, a project, rather than an unproblematic given, obvious in its sheer thereness.

To see what such a politics might begin to look like, we will take three privileged sites of micro-modernity, mobility, digital communication and urbanization and explore how these sites can begin to point the way to a new way of appropriating our experience of the planet.

Mobility

When Italo Calvino's Mr Palomar enters a cheese shop in Paris he is enchanted by what he finds:

> Behind every cheese there is a pasture of different green under a different sky: meadows caked with the salt the tides of Normandy deposit every evening; meadows scented with aromas in the windy sunlight of Provence; there are different flocks with their stablings and their transhumances; there are secret processes handed down over centuries. This shop is a museum: Mr Palomar visiting it, feels, as he does in the Louvre, behind every displayed object the presence of the civilization that has given it form and takes form from it.'
> (Calvino 1986: 66)

A random visit to a Parisian shop becomes a dramatic journey through space and time.

A local shop becomes a secular stargate, a portal into the geography and history of an entire nation. Palomar's epiphany gives vivid expression to a distinction set up by the French travel theorist Jean-Didier Urbain between exotic travel and endotic travel (Urbain 1998: 217-232). Exotic travel is defined as the more conventional mode of thinking about travel where travel is seen to involve leaving the prosaic world of the everyday for a distant place, even if the notion of 'distance' can vary through time. Exotic travel implies leaving familiar surroundings for a place which is generally situated at some remove from the routine world of the traveller. From the perspective of macro-modernity, where far becomes ever nearer through improvements in forms of transportation, it becomes all the more commonplace to equate travel with going far. Endotic travel, on the other hand, is an exercise in staying close by, not leaving the familiar and travelling interstitially through a world we thought we knew. Endotic travel is, in a sense, the mobile site of micro-modernity.

There are three different strands informing the practice of endotic travel. The first strand is the exploration of what Georges Perec has called the 'infra-ordinary' (Perec 1989). Perec explores the teeming detail of confined spaces in works such as *Espèces d'Espaces* (1974) published in English as *Species of spaces and Other Pieces* (2008) and *Tentative d'épuisement d'un lieu parisien* (1982) which appeared in English under the title of *An Attempt at Exhausting a Place in Paris* (2010). In *Species of Spaces*, the narrative focus moves from the bed to the bedroom to the apartment to the apartment building to the street to the town and eventually to the cosmos. In this reverse Google map, the cursor of the writerly eye pulls back from spatial minutiae to a picture which is constructed on a larger and larger scale. However, the primary aim of Perec's method is to make evident the sheer scale of the 'infra-ordinary', the encyclopedic density of things going on in our immediate surrounding which generally pass unnoticed, as is evident in *An Attempt at Exhausting a Place in Paris* where the narrator compulsively lists all the goings on in and around the Café de la Mairie near the Saint Sulpice church in Paris,

The second strand is an ethnology of proximity expressed in a tradition of writing which goes from Montesquieu's *Persian Letters* (1721) to Marc Augé's *La Traversée du Luxembourg* (1985) and *Un Ethnologue dans le métro* (1986) (English translation, *In the Metro* (2002)) . In this ethnographic practice, the usual poles of enquiry are reversed so that it is the domestic not the foreign which becomes the focus of analytic enquiry. In Montesquieu's famous conceit, he presents French society and mores as if they were being observed from the viewpoint of Persian visitors. The familiar is exoticized through this foreignizing practice and along the way the French writer points up the disturbing shortcomings of a putatively 'civilized' society. Marc Augé, for his part, treats the Parisian underground or a Parisian municipal park as if they were an unknown and hitherto unexplored ethnographic terrain; familiar worlds rendered other through the probing inquisitiveness of the professional ethnographer.

The third strand contributing to endotic travel practices is interstitial travel writing. Interstitial travel writing makes its point of departure, its point of arrival. One of the earliest examples is Xavier de Maistre's *Voyage autour de ma chambre* ('Voyage around my Room' (1794)). In this account de Maistre treats his bedroom in Paris as if it were a vast, uncharted and perilous territory where moving from his bed to a chair has all the adventure of an expedition on the high seas. A more recent example is François Maspero's *Les Passagers du Roissy Express* (1990), translated in English as *Roissy Express: a journey through the Paris suburbs* (1994). In this travel account Maspero spends two months with the photographer Anaïk Frantz doing a journey that normally takes forty-five minutes. They stop off at each of the stations on the way to central Paris and what are revealed are whole, other worlds normally invisible to the traveler hurtling through seemingly featureless spaces on the way from the airport to the city.

What these different strands share is that they are all strategies of defamiliarization. They compel the reader to look afresh, to call into question the taken for granted, to take on board the infinitely receding complexity of the putatively routine or prosaic. They suggest that shrinkage is not a matter of scale but of vision. Worlds do not so much shrink as our vision of them. A narrowing of focus, a reduction in scale can in fact lead to an expansion of insight, an unleashing of interpretive and imaginative possibilities often smothered by the large-scale, long-range hubris of the macro-modern.

What endotic travel might involve in routine, everyday life is best captured in Stuart Hall's notion of 'vernacular cosmopolitanism' (Hall 2002: 30). Hall argues that the most notable shift in societies in many parts of the globe in the latter half of the twentieth century has been the rapid, internal differentiation of societies. In other words, whereas formerly, the foreign, the exotic, the other, was held to be over the border or beyond the mountains or over the sea, now the other is next door, or across the street or in the same office. Hall's claims need to historically nuanced as writers such as Charles Bayly have pointed out that versions of vernacular cosmopolitanism have existed in various societies and civilizations down through centuries (Bayly 2004: 1-21). However, the scale and constancy of globalized patterns of migration in more recent times and the creation of supra-national structures like the European Union have meant that a great many places, in particular, but not only, cities, are host to peoples with many different linguistic and cultural backgrounds. This, indeed, is one of the most salient features in Maspero's decelerated odyssey through the stations on the line from Roissy airport to the city centre. He comes into contact with migrants speaking a plurality of languages and bringing with them a variety of spoken and unspoken histories. They are bearers of what James Clifford has called 'travel stories' which he distinguishes from 'travel literature in the bourgeois sense' (Clifford 1992: 110). The stories are multiple in expression and different in origin but crucially they are close to hand. Slowing down involves an opening up. The stories are unlikely to be listened to, however, if there is no language in which they can be understood. This is where the notion of translation comes into play at a social level. As the neighbourhoods of global cities become more densely invested with the linguistic diversity of migrant populations, it is the polylinguals who can facilitate the expression of voices on the endotic travels but only, of course, if they have access to the political means and the cultural resources to make this happen. So what endotic practices reveal are the potentially endless complexity of the everyday lifeworld but also the challenge for a politics of microspection of making this richness an available resource for humanity. We will examine in a later chapter the specific arrangements which would underpin such a politics but we now wish to consider the second site of micro-modernity, digital communication.

Digital worlds

There is more than one way of making voices heard and crucial to how we conceive of a sustainable future for humanity is the role of machine-human interaction. One of the most notable developments in the last two decades has been the shift from stand-alone PCs, located at fixed work stations to the spread of distributed computing in the form of laptops, wireless PDAs, mobile phones with internet connectivity and so on. It is not only humans but their machines which are on the move. As Dennis and Urry express it:

> This trend in distributed computing is developing towards a shift to ubiquitous computing where associations between people, place/space, and time are embedded within a systemic relationship between a person and their kinetic environment. (Dennis and Urry 2007: 13)

Ubiquitous computing sometimes referred to as the 'third wave of computing' is one 'whose cross-over point with personal computing will be around 2005-2020' and which may become 'embedded in walls, chairs, clothing, light switches, cars – in everything' (Brown and Weiser 1996). Greenfield has talked of 'everyware' where information processing is embedded in the objects and surfaces of everyday life (Greenfield 2006: 18). The probable social impact of everyware can be compared to electricity which passes invisibly through the walls of every home, office and car. The transition from fixed locations of access to increased wireless presence coupled with the exponential growth of internet capability means that greatly augmented information flows become part of an information-immersive environment.

A consequence of the emergence of ubiquitous computing is that computing capacity dissolves into the physical surroundings, architectures and infrastructures. Marcos Novak has developed the term 'transArchitecture' to signify 'a liquid architecture that is transmitted across the global information networks; within physical space it exists as an invisible electronic double superimposed on our material world' (Novak 2009) William Mitchell in the 1990s had already spoken of a 'city of bits' where the combination of physical structures in urban spaces with electronic spaces and telematics would be known as 'recombinant architectures' (Mitchell 1995: 46-105).

Implicit in transArchitecture is a dual notion of space, the space of the built physical infrastructure and the virtual spaces of ubiquitous computing. In other words, any point in physical space can open up into the continuously expanded spaces, say, of internet connectivity. The micro-spaces of the transArchitectural become portals not bolt-holes. Any point in physical space is doubled by a potential point of entry into the vastness of computer networks. Advances in peer-to-peer computing and the semantic web further favour the transition from a notion of information provision as available in parallel series to information as part of a networked system, a potentially integrated nexus. In other words, to take the example again of language provision in the multilingual city, rather than content being rolled out in a static, sequential manner (e.g. information leaflets in individual languages at tourist attractions); translated material can be personalised, user-driven and integrated into a dynamic system of ubiquitous delivery.

So it is possible to conceive, for example, of buildings - government offices, university halls of residence, transport hubs – which are multilingually enabled. A hand-held device, such as a mobile phone, allows the user to access relevant information in the language of his or her choice. Thus, rather than the static and serial presentation of information in a limited number of languages, such a development allows for a customised inter-action with the language user with the possibility for continuous expansion in languages offered and information offered.

Such developments are in line with the four dominant ideas for the future as articulated by the UK Foresight Report: Personal Mobility; Cyberspace; Smart Flows; and Urban Environment (Sharpe and Hodgson 2006). More specifically, the trans-architec-tural dimension to the development of physical space underlines the importance of digital communication as a constituent element of micro-modernity. In any consideration of the promises of ubiquitous computing it is, of course, necessary to be wary of the hubristic excess of cyber-rhetoric and be mindful of shop worn digital fantasies such as the 'paperless office'. However, what is worth noting is that ubiquitous computing adds another element to the practice of endotic travel, there now being two dimensions through which the traveller moves, the physical and the virtual. There is a further dimension to the experience of micro-modernity which must be considered and this is our third site, urbanization.

Urbanization

As we noted earlier, one notable consequence of the coming together of migration and accelerated urbanization is the complexification of the language and cultural realities of cities and here we will look at this complexification in the context of the micro-modern. A positive construction of language otherness in urban settings is to see linguistic otherness as an area of genuine possibility, bringing with it new perspectives, energies, traditions and forms of expression into a society, opening up the micro-spaces of modernity to endotic exploration. This, of course, begs the question as to how this positive view of alterity might be realized in view of the sheer language diversity of contemporary migration and the prevalence of elite language ideologies which see diversity as a problem or more prosaically, as a cost. Here again it is worth considering the contemporary city as a site of micro- rather than macro-modernity and examine the consequences for a politics of microspection. Richard Sennett claims, for example, that the major contemporary problem for urbanists 'how do you intensify rather than localize social interaction?' (Sennett 2002: 47). In other words, how do you get people to live together, rather than simply co-exist together? How is it possible to avoid large gatherings of citizens from becoming a cluster of multiple solitudes? Is the only viable option taking refuge in the exclusive enclave of community?

One way of addressing Sennett's question is to consider multilingual, multi-ethnic urban space as first and foremost a *translation zone*. In other words, if translation is primarily about a form of interaction with another language and culture (which in turn modifies one's own), then it is surely to the notion of translation that we must look if we want to think about how the micro-spaces of global neighbourhoods might become something other than the regime of non-interactive indifference decried by Sennett.

China, for example, intends to move 400 million people, which is roughly half of the country's rural population, into urban centres by 2030 (Dennis and Urry 2007: 10). The urbanisation of the population is the rule rather than the exception in contemporary demographic developments and indeed the nature and extent of urbanisation has exercised many commentators from Jacobs to Sassen (Jacobs 1962; Sassen 2006)). Part of the impetus for the drive to urbanisation is the ecological imperative of using resources efficiently by having people come together in one place rather than having them living in scattered dwellings with ecologically onerous infrastructural costs. In addressing issues of urban development, town planners ritually concern themselves with problems of traffic management, the state of public utilities, the availability of parking and green spaces, the viability of urban communities, the sustainability of waste practices and so on but it seems inexplicable that the multi-lingual composition of cities across the planet as it effects planning decisions is generally ignored or treated as best as a peripheral issue (see Campbell and Fainstein 2003). The lacuna is all the more surprising in that language difference is the most immediate, audible and practical sign of the presence of others. Most notably, it is language difference which signals the micro-complexity of the urban space, a complexity that challenges the macro-narratives of urban management where if language figures at all it is as a 'cost', the contemporary epithet for anything that is construed as a problem by elite groups. More worryingly, the failure to recognise the complex linguistic and cultural hinterland of the micro-spaces of urban communities leads to the emergence of unhealthy alliances between stereotype and rejectionist purism. In 2008, the European Commission against Racism and Intolerance noted in its Third Report on the Netherlands (2008) that it had 'received an increasing number of reports according to which racial profiling (i.e. the use, with no objective and reasonable justification of grounds such as race, colour, language, religion, nationality or national or ethnic origin in control, surveillance and other similar law enforcement activities) is not uncommon in the Netherlands' (European Commission against Racism and Intolerance 2007). Given that language tests are now a central and public part of citizenship requirements in countries such as the Netherlands, Denmark and the United Kingdom, it is hardly surprising that racial profiling should find an alibi in a systematic distrust of language difference. Indeed, the very attempt to negotiate that difference has been identified by certain commentators in the United Kingdom as a dangerous abettor of civic disloyalty:

It's a shocking figure: more than £100m was spent in the past year on translating and interpreting for British residents who don't speak English. In the name of multiculturalism, one Home Office-funded centre alone provides these services in 76 languages[…]The financial cost is bad enough, but there is a wider problem about the confused signals we are sending to immigrant communities. We are telling them they don't have to learn English, let alone integrate. Worse by isolating them linguistically, we have created communities that are now incubators for islamo-fascism. (Rahman 2006)

The paradigm underlying these comments is an assimilationist paradigm which sees all newcomers and residents as translated into the dominant language of the host community, the macro-idiom of the macro-space. It is a unidirectional, binary conception of translation which adjudges the nature of translation to be *either* one thing *or* the other. Either everybody speaks the macro-target language or everyone is condemned to the fractious babble of micro-languages, colonizing the micro-spaces (and eventually the macro-space) of the city. Such a scenario is ultimately grounded in the worldview of macro-modernity which can only conceive of difference as oppositional. In other words, if a target language, for example, is to be dominant then the very existence of source languages is a threat to the hegemony of the One.

Arjun Appadurai in his exploration of large-scale violence against minorities in Eastern Europe, Rwanda and India in the 1990s speaks of the 'anxiety of incompleteness'. His argument is that numerical majorities can become violent, even genocidal towards 'small numbers' when minorities remind majorities of the 'small gap which lies between their conditions as majorities and the horizon of an unsullied national whole, a pure and untainted national ethos' (Appadurai 2006: 8). Such movements become particularly prevalent in times of rapid change where national economies and welfare systems are made fragile by the globalization of financial and market relationships:

> The virtually complete loss of even the fiction of a national economy, which had some evidence for its existence in the eras of strong socialist states and central planning now leaves the cultural field as the main one in which fantasies of purity, authenticity, borders, and security can be enacted. (22-23)

States which are invited to open themselves to the flows of Western capital and the ministrations of transnational corporations compensate by acting out dramas of national sovereignty in the cultural arena. Hence, the prevalence of moral panic around foreign migrants, foreign customs, foreign beliefs and foreign languages and the suspicion around cities as sites of subversive micro-modernity, as pockets of resistance that must be cleansed of their difference.

In positing the city as translation zone we are arguing for a different paradigmatic representation of the contemporary city, the city as a legitimate expression of micro-modernity. The fundamental move is to see translation as an analog, both/and praxis which allows for *both* the instrumental utility of target language translation, the engagement with the larger, macrospaces *and* the pragmatic and cultural necessity of mother-tongue maintenance, the cultivation and celebration of micro-sensitivity and sensibility. To take just one example, integration is not all about either English, for example, or nothing else. As the evidence of countless countries throughout the world attests, it is perfectly possible for human beings to operate in more than one language at any number of different levels (Edwards 1995). In this respect, due attention to the practice of translation and the encouragement of language diversity in societies is to do nothing that is particularly exceptional in global terms but it is to do something that is deeply enriching in local contexts.

Crucial to the use of the notion of translation in the micro-spaces of the city is a contention that language (and by extension cultural difference) should not be seen as 'barrier' or an 'obstacle' but as an opportunity. Implicit in this conception is polylingualism rather than monolingualism. If multilingualism suggests a serial image of discrete units, polylingualism implies a more open, networked form of language relationships. Translators are, by definition, polylinguals, but in the repeated representations of cities as sites of serial monolingualism the role of polylinguals is minimised or forgotten. The reformulation of public space in urban centres as primarily a translation zone, a privileged site of micro-modernity has the potential to promote a model of social cohesion which promotes the inclusion not the elimination of difference. So in everything from small local theatres presenting translations of plays from different migrant languages to new voice recognition and speech synthesis technology producing discrete translations in wireless environments to systematic client education for community interpreting to translation workshops as part of diversity management courses in the workplace, the possibilities for a more dynamic, micro and less hegemonic, macro conception of urban centres are numerous. What such an approach implies is the calling into question of the distinction between elite polylingualism and remedial polylingualism. That is to say whereas a particular language repertoire involving traditional modern European languages (French, German, Spanish) and more recently, Mandarin Chinese can be viewed as a positive attribute for managerial staff in transnational corporations (elite polylingualism), a language repertoire comprising the Urdu, Arabic and Albanian of migrants competing for bottom-rung service sector jobs can be construed as an impediment to integration which must be managed away by assimilative strategies in the social and educational services (remedial polylingualism). In challenging the implied distinction between one form of polylingualism that is perceived as prestigious and desirable and another form which is presented as alien and threatening, the construction of the city as translation zone allows for a form of dynamic cohesion which promotes not excludes the local. More generally the specific case of language diversity and translation shows how the local need not be confining and how endotic practices are expansionist rather than reductionist.

If cohesion is a watchword of civic viability, sustainability is the mantra of ecological survival and a central concern of any long-term notion of what is said to be viable. The Scottish theorist Alastair McIntosh describes a 'cycle of belonging' which he sees as integral to any notion of the sustainable. The cycle has four elements which follow on from each other, a sense of place (grounding) which gives rise to a sense of identity (ego/head) that carries with it a sense of values (soul/heart) which generates in turn a sense of responsibility (action/hand) (McIntosh 2008: 235). In emphasising the role of place, McIntosh is trying to formulate a basis for collective togetherness and responsibility which has an inclusive civic basis rather than an exclusive ethnic basis. The concern with place has equally pressing pragmatic concerns which are to do with the sustainability of human communities. As he points out, for humans to live like the average Indian, half a planet would be needed, to live like an average European, three would be needed, and to live like the average American, seven planets would be required. McIntosh concludes that 'It is only if we can find fulfilment in close proximity to one another and local place that we can hope to stop sucking what we need from all over the world' (71-2).

It is the disconnection from place where agricultural land is drained, rivers are straightened and concrete is poured over ground that once served as a vital sponge, which leads to the catastrophic flooding in Indonesia, Africa, India, England and elsewhere, aggravated by increased rainfall due to climate change. The disconnection is not without agency, of course, and much of the environmental damage is justified by the alibis of 'progress' and 'development'. But fundamental to any ethics of sustainability or cycle of belonging must be an understanding of place not only as an object in space but as a phenomenon in time. By this we mean there is a further dimension to the city as translation zone which resides not only in the social (community interpreting) or the technological (ubiquitous computing) but in the historical.

The historical dimension fundamentally relates to the role of a particular kind of history in re-presenting stories of place. In tracing histories of contact and exchange in urban settings, cultural historians such as Sherry Simon, show that any proper or fuller understanding of place involves bringing to light the multiple, embedded stories of how language communities have negotiated their relationships through translation down through the centuries (Simon 2006). In other words, what is made apparent is that places have a multiplicity of origins and what contemporary migratory developments bring to the fore is the buried multiple histories of specific places. For example, Timothy Brook in *Vermeer's Hat: The 17th Century and the Dawn of the Global World* draws on the material objects found in Vermeer's paintings (a beaver fur hat, a china bowl) to chart the relationship between Dutch cities and forms of proto-global-ization (Brook 2008). The objects are used as evidence to show how local lives were intensely connected with and affected by currents of migration, exchange and influence. The need for beaver fur by European milliners will have a decisive effect on the nature of the French colonization of Canada in much the same way as Dutch appetites for Chinese porcelain will have significant consequences for its domestic manufacturing industry and the financial structures of its trading arrangements. This is not to suggest that major developments in world trade are simply a question of giving customers what they want but points to the long-range consequences of the manufacture of desire through fashion, desire for social mobility or changes in the function of domestic spaces in Early Modern Europe (Rybzinski 1986). In a sense, what emerges here is an endotic form of history writing which explores the local place for its connections outwards, its inter-dependence on other languages, cultures, places. Allowing for this approach invests place with a form of fractal complexity which is central to the model of micro-modernity. Highlighting the historical dimension has the added advantage of providing a historical 'home' to newcomers in that they are made aware of the fact that many places have been places of passage and interchange and that their very 'newness' is part of a long tradition of arrival and settlement, a micro-challenge to the macro-legends of uniform settlement. But what about the larger 'home', planet earth, and what can micro-modernity tell us about a new ethics of dwelling?

Chapter Two

Denizens

One of the most common icons of the global age is not surprisingly the globe itself. From the shots of the blue planet suspended over abyssal darkness courtesy of the Apollo space missions to the sketchy outline of earth on notices encouraging hotel customers to re-use their towels, the images of the planet are increasingly common in the contemporary imaginary. Seeing things from a distance is as much a matter of subjection as observation. Occupying a superior vantage point from which one can look down on a subject people or a conquered land is a staple of colonial travel narratives (Pratt 1992: 216). There is a further dimension to the question of distance described by Tim Ingold where he draws a distinction between perceiving the environment as a 'sphere' or as a 'globe'. For centuries, the classic description of the heavens was of the earth as a sphere with lines running from the human observer to the cosmos above. As geocentric cosmology fell into discredit and heliocentric cosmology came into the ascendant, the image of the sphere gave way to that of the globe. If the sphere presupposed a world experienced and engaged with from within, the globe represented a world perceived from without. Thus, in Ingold's words, 'the movement from spherical to global imagery is also one in which "the world", as we are taught it exists, is drawn ever further from the matrix of our lived experience' (Ingold 2000: 211).

In the movement towards the modern, a practical sensory engagement with the world underpinned by the spherical paradigm is supplanted by a regimen of detachment and control. As the images of the globe proliferate, often ironically to mobilize ecological awareness, the danger is that these images themselves distort our relationship to our physical and cultural environment by continually situating us at a distance, by abstracting and subtracting us from our local attachments and responsibilities. As Heise observes, 'Given the current intellectual investment in the inherent value of cultural, racial, ethnic, and gender difference, the Blue Planet concept is also an obvious target of criticism for its erasure of political and cultural differences' (Heise 2008: 24) However, it is precisely such an ability which is often construed as a basic requirement for both national and more latterly global citizenship. It is the capacity to look beyond the immediate interests of the clan or village or ethnic grouping which creates the conditions for a broader definitions of belonging at a national or indeed global level. Szersynski and Urry argue, for example, that "banal globalism", the almost unnoticed symbols of globality that crowd our daily lives, might, 'be helping to create a sensibility conducive to the cosmopolitan rights and duties of being a 'global citizen', by generating a greater sense of both global diversity and global interconnectedness and belonging' (Szersynski and Urry 2006: 122). The promise of such citizenship is an almost axiomatic contemporary defence of why anyone should bother with reading literature in other languages. When Pascale Casanova in her survey of the World Republic of Letters tries to synthesize those elements which have conditioned eligibility for citizenship of this Republic of Letters, translation is very much to the fore:

> In the world of literature, if languages can also be represented using a 'floral figure', that is to say a system where languages on the periphery are linked to the centre by polyglots and translators then it is possible to measure the literariness (the power, prestige, the volume of linguistico-literary capital) of a language, not by the number of writers and readers in a language, but by the number of literary polyglots (or main

players in the literary arena, publishers, cosmopolitan inter-
mediaries, well-educated talent spotters...) who know it and
by the number of literary translators – for export as well as for
import – who cause texts to be translated into or out of this
literary language. (Casanova 1999 : 37)[1]

The global standing of a literature, for example, depends on the
efforts of those language learners and translators who can stand
outside their own language and learn the other language for the
purposes of reading and/or written translation. But Szersynski
and Urry ask the following questions, 'is this abstraction from
the local and particular fully compatible with dwelling in a
locality? Could it be that the development of a more
cosmopolitan, citizenly perception of place is at the expense of
other modes of appreciating and caring for local environments
and contexts?' (Szersynski and Urry 2006: 123).

In opposition to the figure of the citizen we find the notion of
the 'denizen' which has been propagated notably by the non-
governmental organisation Common Ground. A denizen is
deemed to be a person who dwells in a particular place and who
can move through and knowingly inhabit that place. The word
originates in the Latin dē intus (from within) which mutates into
Old French deinzein-deinz (modern French dans). What is
compelling about the term is that it both espouses a relationship
to place (a knowing from within) and a flexibility in terms of
adoption and adaptability as among the dictionary definitions
listed for 'denizen' are 'one admitted to the rights of a citizen: a
wild plant, probably foreign, that keeps its footing: a naturalised
foreign word' (Kirkpatrick 1983: 332:333). Therefore, Common
Ground dedicates itself to encouraging the proliferation of
vernacular, ideographic and connotative descriptions of local
places which can take the form of place myths, stories, personal
associations and celebrations of various kinds and these descriptions are widely varied in origin (www.commonground.org.uk).

The importance of the concept of denizenship as part of a politics of microspection will be discussed in the different but related contexts of tourism, real estate and migration.

Sightseeing

An inevitable consequence of banal globalism is the tyranny of the gaze. Martin Heidegger's claim that the 'fundamental act of the modern age is the conquest of the world as picture' is hardly surprising given the centrality of seeing to the rise of Western science (Heidegger 1977: 134). Relying on the testimony of the eyes rather than the authority of texts became the touchstone of the new scientific method championed by Francis Bacon and others (Rorty 1980). The importance of ocularcentrism was relayed by the development and enhancement of optical instruments such as the microscope and telescope. Literacy and the advent of printing gave further impetus to visualised and spatialised perceptions of experience (Ong 1989). In more recent times, the process of commodification itself has a strong visual correlate as noted by Eamonn Slater:

> As the process of commodification penetrates deeper into the cultural realms of society, commodity production takes on a more visual character: this corresponds to a process of *visualisation*. Images and visual symbols become the universal language of commodity production across national boundaries. Television, movies and the advertising industry can replicate images endlessly and beam them virtually anywhere (his emphasis). (Slater 1998: 4)

This has profound implications not only for goods and services, the usual focus of discussions around the design-intensity of aestheticized goods such as branded clothing and rock music (de Zengotita 2005), but for the very 'common ground' on which people rest.

One of the salient features of experience in the developed world is the emergence of a comparative cartographic gaze based on the twin imperatives of tourism and real estate. As the world opened up to travellers in the second half of the twentieth century and tourism rapidly became one of the most important items of trade on the planet, the range of potential destinations increased significantly (Urry 1990). The ending of the Cold War, for example, saw the emergence of many former Soviet bloc countries as prime destinations for tourists as the economies of central and eastern Europe sought to accelerate infrastructural development and employment through tourism. It is no accident in this respect that many of the locations chosen for the shooting of the pioneering James Bond film *Casino Royale* (2006) were to be found in the Czech Republic and Montenegro. When the picturesque locations are to be found in low-wage, low-tax and low-cost environments then film producers and tourism promoters are united in a shared passion for the financial and visual sublime. Destinations through brochures, television travel programmes, magazine articles, Sunday supplements, can be visually compared across the globe. The planet from this carto-graphic perspective becomes a set of juxtaposed images on offer to the viewers or corporations who have the financial where-withal to make choices.

Real Estate
The correlative in real estate is the fate of property in a globalised world. As restrictions on the movement of funds and the acqui-sition of property were relaxed in many countries in the 1980s and 1990s, significant investment funds were directed towards real estate which could now be purchased and evaluated on a worldwide basis. So now in Singapore, it is possible to buy 1000 feet of office space in London and vice versa (Sennet 2002: 46). When N.H. Seek, the President of the real estate firm GIC desig-nates the 'world winning cities' which represent optimal possi-

bilities for property investment, the list includes Calgary, Austin, San José, Helsinki, Tallinn, Budapest, Barcelona, Cape Town, Santiago (Chile), Porto Alegre, Delhi, Mumbai, Bangalore, Xian, Shenzhen, Shanghai, Beijing and Guangzhou (Seek 2006). It is not just pension funds and large corporate investors, however, who seek financial redemption in bricks and mortar.

Dhananjayan Sriskandarajah of the Institute for Public Policy Research noted that in 2004 alone, over 200,000 British nationals left the United Kingdom to live abroad on a long-term or permanent basis. A survey showed that over one-fifth of Britons intended to spend their retirement years abroad and with one quarter of the British population set to reach retirement age by 2030, this means many millions of Britons will be living outside the country in locations dotted across the globe (Sriskandarajah 2006). The popularity of programmes in the UK such as the Channel 4 series 'A Place in the Sun' which helps 'buyers find their dream home in an exotic location' further reinforce this powerful comparative cartographic gaze where the world is flattened into the collage of the holiday snapshot album, except that in the case of property buyers, the holidaymakers do not go away but stay behind. What is striking with this visual instrumentalism whether it be in tourist discourse or real estate is that, '[p]laces have turned into a collection of abstract characteristics, in a mobile world, ever easier to be visited, appreciated and compared, but not known from within' (Szerszynski and Urry 2006: 127). It is in this context that it may be more appropriate to posit as a possible ideal for a politics of microspection not so much an ideal of a *global citizen* as a *global denizen*. In other words, what denizenship posits is a knowledge from within and this knowledge if we consider the aims of Common Ground – place myths, stories, personal associations – is almost invariably though not exclusively expressed through language.

If the slogan of real estate agents is 'Location, Location, Location' there could hardly be a better definition at some level of what people who engage with other languages and cultures do. Part of their business is to understand what people actually say in a particular location and to bring this knowledge to another location, the target language. This is why the education and training of cultural mediators take years. It is not so much an abstraction from as an engagement in local attachments that is demanded by the task and this task takes time. When Richard (Brad Pitt) in *Babel* desperately seeks help for his wife, Susan (Cate Blanchett) who has been inadvertently shot, he shouts out the English word 'Help' to a Moroccan motorist who bewildered and alarmed speeds off. The visual promise of the holiday is undercut by the linguistic reality of his surroundings. The inability to translate foregrounds a cultural blindness on the part of the traveller who finds he is not so much an empowered citizen of the world as the unwilling denizen of a place. In this sense what the failure to translate does is to reinstate the importance of a particular kind of time in overly spatialised and visualised models of the global. The importance of instantaneous time is repeatedly emphasized by commentators on globalization who see the availability of cheap, ubiquitous computing as the portal to a flat world of instant, limitless connectedness (Friedman 2005).

This standard time-space compression thesis of macro-modernity lends itself effectively to panoptic ideals of global simultaneity where the variousness of the world can be captured on a multiplicity of screens. However, this perception is in marked contradiction to the intensely local, place-bound existence of the majority of inhabitants on the planet. Gerladine Pratt and Susan Hanson, for example, argue that:

Although the world is increasingly well connected, we must hold this in balance with the observation that most people live intensely local lives; their homes, work places, recreation, shopping, friends, and often family are all located within a relatively small orbit. The simple and obvious fact that overcoming distance requires time and money means that the everyday events of daily life are well grounded within a circumscribed arena. (Pratt and Hanson 1994: 10-11)

This is not to argue, of course, that place cannot be shaped by influences from elsewhere, even if people do not move. On the contrary, from the spread of Buddhism in China to the initiation of rural electrification projects worldwide, local lives can be dramatically transformed by developments which have their point of origin many thousands of kilometres away. What the prevalence of local lives does mean, however, is that local languages, local cultures, local habituses, local ways of relating to surrounding environments, have a reality which resists the easy sweep of the comparative cartographic gaze.

Chrono-diversity

A further implication is that an idea of durational time must be invoked alongside the more commonly represented notion of instantaneous time. The chrono-diversity of the planet cannot be reduced to the single experience of time of a particular form of macro-modernity which sees itself as everywhere, and all-seeing, all at once. That is to say, any notion of an understanding of another culture, many of which in a multilingual world involve another language, implies a potential three-phase level of translational interaction which is at the constituent core of denizenship and durational time. Phase One interaction is heteronomous translation which involves relying on someone to do the translation for you, whether it is the interpreter in the real estate office in France or the Polish PA negotiating for the foreign business person with local suppliers in Warsaw. Interpreting, no matter how proficient, takes time and already there is a sense in which time is beginning to 'thicken' in phase one translation exchange. Phase Two is the shift towards semi-autonomous translation where subjects want to begin to learn the language themselves and in a sense do their own translation. They begin to invest a certain amount of time in the process so that the durational reality of time begins to take precedence over the instantaneous. Alison Phipps in *Learning the Arts of Linguistic Survival* (2007) describes the experiences of 'tourist language learners' based in Scotland learning foreign languages and she demonstrates how tourists' perception of time and place alters with the shift to semi-autonomous translation. The place of instant escape mutates into the longer time of discovery. Phase Three is full-autonomous translation where subjects become fully functioning bilinguals or polylinguals whose competence involves extensive investment of time either as a result of circumstance (being brought up in bilingual/multilingual environments) or acquisition (formal language study). In Phase Three, the act of translating takes less time but, of course, the period of time necessary to acquire the skill is often extensive. All three phases involve the growing acknowledgement of the state of denizenship with the shift from the heteronomous to the autonomous modes of translation indicating a gradual shift from recognition to implication. Put simply, engagement with another language and culture involves an increasing implication in the placedness of that language and culture. All three phases imply the gradual restoration of durational time as a dimension to the experience and understanding of space as the dwelling of the denizen is not only an operation in space (living in a particular place) but a function of time (living there for a particular period of time). What the inevitable fact of this understanding of translation contests in a sense is the banal globalism which draws the world in Ingold's words cited earlier 'ever further from the matrix of our lived experience'. One facet of that lived experience is the acknowledgement of the existence of an elite and remedial polylingualism mentioned in chapter one and the necessity for translation in all three phases to apply to all languages, and not just those with high social and cultural capital.

One of the fundamental misunderstandings of the new 'flat-earthers' in their euphoric celebration of a friction-free globalisation is to substitute distance as a physical fact for distance as an economic reality. To present the world as a smaller place because planes fly faster or computer messages are delivered at greater speed is to assume that proximity is a function of time and closeness is simply a matter of real or virtual cohabitation. However, distance for human beings is primarily social rather than physical (Massey 2004). In other words, living near to or close to someone does not imply that contact is therefore immediate, instantaneous and unproblematic because matters of income, class, gender may make any meeting or interaction a distinctly remote possibility. To take one example out of many, Michael Förster, David Jesuit and Timothy Smeeding in their study of regional poverty and income inequality in Central and Eastern Europe in the period after the collapse of the Soviet bloc noted a marked and continuous rise in income inequalities as the economies of the region became increasingly integrated into the global economy. They further observed that in the case of the Czech Republic, Hungary and Poland, income inequality tended to be particularly marked in the capital cities (Förster, Jesuit and Smeeding 2003). So as the world's economy drew closer, the income disparities between citizens of the same territories grew larger. The physical proximity to a global network economy was enhanced but the social distance between groups was increased. The social nature of distance is a vivid illustration of the realities of denizenship which may be very much at variance with more abstracted or detached notions of citizenship with its accompanying utopia of friction-free possibility. Distance as a socio-economic construction also underlines the necessity for integrating questions of power into a politics of microspection as near to hand is not always close to heart. Nowhere is this more vividly illustrated than in the domain of immigration that we touched on earlier.

Migration

In 2005, the United Population Division projected that in the period 2005-2050 the net number of international migrants to more developed regions would be around 98 million. In the period 2000-2005, net immigration in twenty-eight countries either prevented population decline or at least doubled the contribution of natural increase (births minus deaths) to population growth (United Nations Population Division 2005). Two main contributory factors to increased migration are of course ageing populations in wealthier countries and the huge labour demands of service-intensive economies (Sassen 1999). Thus the combined effects of demographic disparity and the exponential growth of the tertiary sector in developed economies means the demands for economic migrants, despite the vociferations of political parties on the Far Right, are set to continue, if not increase. As many migrants are brought in initially, at any rate, to perform poorly-paid, relatively unskilled jobs, the sense of social distance can be relatively acute as the affluent diners in the upmarket restaurant will have little in common with the migrant kitchen help working only a few steps way behind closed doors.

The distance can of course be even more marked in that what the increasingly global search for migrant workers has done, despite the many obstacles put in place by national governments, is to alter the linguistic composition of workforces. Bischoff and Loutan, for example, reporting on the interpreting situation in Swiss hospitals noted the consequences for translation and language awareness of a shift in migration patterns. In earlier decades, migrants had largely come from countries that spoke a Romance language such as Portuguese, Spanish and Italian. Towards the end of the last century, the situation began to change and they found in a nationwide survey of interpreter

services in Swiss hospitals that the languages requiring inter-
preters were amongst others, Albanian, South Slavic (Serbian,
Croatian, Bosnian, Slovenian, Macedonian, Bulgarian), Turkish,
Tamil, Kurdish, Arabic and Russian (Bischoff and Loutan 2004:
191). Thus, there was a shift from relatively low levels of
linguistic awareness due to a real or assumed familiarity with
cognate Romance languages to a situation where radical
linguistic dissimilarity made the fact and existence of language
otherness inescapable. Hence, the recourse to language
mediation in the hospitals was the acknowledgement of distance
and the need to bridge this distance in some way.

Tollefson in his study of Indochinese refugees working in the
United States showed how difficult it may be for migrants to
integrate into a host community. His subjects working long,
unsocial hours in poorly paid, largely unskilled jobs had few
opportunities to meet or socialise with Anglophone co-workers.
An inability to communicate in the dominant host language or to
translate what has been said often compounded a situation of
isolation and exploitation (Tollefson 1989). Therefore, when
growing multiculturalism is presented as evidence of a shrinking
planet or versions of vernacular cosmopolitanism are offered as
incontrovertible proof of the emergence of the global village, it is
necessary to understand the socio-economic dimension to
distance and the increasing linguistic hybridity of migrant
workforces to restore a proper sense of complexity to place in
globalized settings. More significantly, from the perspective of
micro-modernity, the proper understanding of what it is to be a
denizen in a particular locality in the context of global mobility
(and immobility) makes the task of nuanced analysis more rather
than less important. In other words, accelerated mobility rather
than continuously smoothing out differences in the sense of the
frictionless circulation of a global economy of signs and spaces
makes the presence of endotic complexity even more apparent. A
politics of microspection involves the return of the repressed

detail of spherical situatedness to debates too often dominated by the visual shorthand of the global paradigm.

Macro/micro

How we see the world then is part of how we see ourselves. But how we see the world is also bound up with how we represent the world to ourselves and how we believe we understand it. Edwin R. Tufte in *Envisioning Information* discusses Constantine Anderson's precise axonometric projection of midtown Manhattan. Anderson in his map was partly going back to the cartographic tradition exemplified by Michel Etienne Turgot and Louis Bretez *Plan de Paris* where the very precise rendering of every façade and building in the city of Paris allows the reader to literally wander through the streets of the map while still being afforded the bird's-eye view that the overall *Plan* provides. In Tuftes's comments on Anderson's map, he argues:

> This fine texture of exquisite detail leads to personal micro-readings, individual stories about the data: shops visited, hotels stayed at, walks taken, office windows at a floor worked on – all in the extended context of an entire building, street and neighbourhood. Detail accumulates into large coherent structures; those thousands of tiny windows, when seen at a distance, gray into surfaces to form a whole building. Simplicity of reading derives from the context of detailed and complex information, properly arranged. A most unconventional design strategy is revealed: *to clarify, add detail.* (his emphasis) (Tufte 1990: 37)

It is possible therefore to develop both highly personal detailed readings and to perceive larger structures of coherence.

A similar process is at work in the Vietnam Veterans Memorial in Washington D.C. where from a distance the viewer sees a long continuous rectangle of black granite. Coming closer to the memorial it is possible to pick out individual names and for those who have lost friends or relatives the individual names carry with them their own specific stories and resonance. Tufte asserts that a fundamental and effective principle of information design is at work in these micro/macro compositions. What the panorama or the vista does is to give the viewer the freedom of choice that comes with the overview, the ability to compare and sort through detail. On the other hand, the 'micro-information, like smaller texture in landscape perception, provides a credible refuge where the space of visualisation is condensed, slowed, personalized' (38). In these high-density designs viewers select, narrate and recast data for their own purposes. One viewer might see the Veterans Memorial as a visually overwhelming indictment of warfare and empire whereas another might see the mention of a loved one as a fitting tribute to patriotic sacrifice for a noble cause. In macro/micro designs it is the viewers rather than the designers or editors who are in control of the information. There is in a sense no predicting or dictating to what uses the designs will be put. Moreover as Tufte notes: 'Data-thin, forgetful displays move viewers towards ignorance and passivity, and at the same time diminish the credibility of the source' (50). The less data there is available, the more viewers are likely to wonder what has been left out and for what reason. In other words, clarification does not always imply reduction and simplification can simply mean mystification.

Simpleness of data and design does not automatically imply clarity of reading, '[s]impleness is another aesthetic preference, not an information display strategy, not a guide to clarity. What we seek instead is a rich texture of data, a comparative context, an understanding of complexity revealed with an economy of means' (51). In a sense, what is being argued for here is a way of visualising the world that does not succumb to the panoramic sweep of mastery but that makes complexity a condition of interpretive freedom. The less subtle and complex the account, the less interesting the reading. If we relate the notion of micro/macro designs back to the discussion of migration, tourism and real estate, then what we find as an emergent thread is the connection between the micro-information of actual human settings and the potential overview of a politics of microspection.

Robert Venturi writing on complexity and contradiction in architecture observed that, 'an architecture of complexity and contradiction has a special obligation towards the whole: its truth must be in its totality or its implication of totality. It must embody the difficult unity of inclusion rather than the easy unity of exclusion[...]Less is a bore' (Venturi 1977: 17). Even if totality is a term that almost invariably provokes unease and is rarely available as a hermeneutic possibility in the human and social sciences, the gesturing towards the 'difficult unity of inclusion' is important. Here a difficulty of inclusion is not to be understood in terms of closure but as precisely a movement, however difficult, to include more not exclude.

Invoking notions of denizenship, durational time and spherical situatedness is part of this movement but it also helps to shift an exclusive emphasis in historical analysis from the transnational to the *translocational*. A notable feature of contemporary historiography is the emergence of 'global history' which crosses national frontiers, takes a long-term perspective, is comparative in spirit, draws on several disciplines and is particularly interested in questions of contact, exchange, hybridity and migration (Testot 2009: 7-8). Global history has the signal merit of contesting the dominance of the nation-state paradigm in the writing of the histories of national polities, languages, literatures and cultures. The history of nations is no longer be understood as a *sui generis*, internal development within immutably fixed borders but is presented increasingly as the result of an intense traffic of influences from elsewhere. The emphasis on the transnational also complements, of course, the accelerated flows of goods, peoples and services commonly associated with the emergence of globalisation in late macro-modernity.

There may be a sense, however, in which an undue attention to the transnational still leaves analysts operating within the implicit paradigm of the national (if only in terms of scale) and that what is required is smaller-scale, more spatially located and temporally durational forms of enquiry such as the model provided by Sherry Simon's *Translating Montreal* (2006). In her exploration of one specific city and the manner in which the denizens of the city over time have engaged with the fact of political and cultural difference, Simon shows not only how detail clarifies but how from an endotic perspective it is possible to conceive of a politics of place beyond place. That is to say, concentration on one particular place becomes an opening out rather than a closing down, a foregrounding of a complexity of connectedness to other cultures, languages, histories, rather than a paean to singular insularity. Norman Davies and Roger Moorhouse's history of Wroclaw equally shows the macro/micro design of inward/outward connexity in the centuries-old history of one location (Davies and Moorhouse 2002). Translocational analyses of place invite us to revisit assumptions about the nature of space and time in recent and not so recent human history. They also, more urgently, cause us to consider the consequences for places where people live of the failure to take cognisance of the full complexity of the intensely localized arenas of human interaction.

In considering human interaction it goes without saying that we need to consider the nature of the beings involved in the interaction. To this end, it is worth shifting the endotic perspective of micro-modernity from the externalities of place to the internalities of the people inhabiting these places.

Conflict

A substantial part of bookshops in many richer countries is given over to self-help manuals. Implicit in these manuals is the notion that there is an ideal self which is somewhat out of kilter because it lacks confidence, vitamin B, the X factor or has failed to dejunk its life. 'I am not myself today' implies that there is a unitary, consensual self which is the desirable default value for the good life. That is to say, reading the right book, taking the right therapy, buying the right product, will lead to the finding of a 'true self' beyond disharmony or conflict. This psychologised consensualism finds its correlative at a political level in the notion that representative democracy consists of a collection of points of view which are all equally valid. The point of view of the workers' representative where 2,000 jobs have been delocalized is as valid as that of the corporate vice-president who has engineered the 'rationalization'. So everybody gets to have their say. But what they are saying is that real conflict is no longer acceptable. In other words, in reality, points of view are irreducible, as speakers are situated very differently, both materially and structurally. The false symmetrization of the mediasphere, however, conceals the very genuine conflict of interests through the irenic fiction of the representative soundbite.

In another version of the tyranny of compliance, when social movements oppose government measures, such as penalizing public sector workers for the financial irresponsibility of the private sector, government spokespersons and stockbroker economists talk about a 'communications deficit.' If only the people understood what they were doing, they would realize it was ultimately for their own good. Opposition can only be conceived of as cussedness or stupidity. No allowance is made for the fact that there are grounded material interests and structural conditions which make opposition not only inevitable but vital. It is in this context that an endotic perspective can be of value to us in proposing a way of thinking about the ontological necessity of conflict.

As even the most rudimentary exercise in the study of others soon reveals, understanding is above all an initiation into unsuspected complexity. The simplest of situations involving other humans turns out to be not as straightforward as we thought. What this schooling in complexity reveals is the radical insufficiency of cultural shorthand. That is to say, the cultural categorisation of society as made of recognisable types designated by labels, 'dyslexic', 'epileptic', 'Paddy', 'Gay', 'Muslim', reduces the multi-dimensional complexity of humans to one defining trait. Once a person is described using one of these labels, it is suggested that is all you need to know about them. They become transparent. Thus, if someone is 'Muslim', they must be by definition, bigoted, anti-modern, misogynist and obscurantist. What gay rights activists and the womens' movement, for example, in various parts of the globe and at different times have attempted to do is to restore multi-dimensionality and complexity to the lives of human beings who were deemed to be instantly intelligible as 'gay' or 'woman', gender or sexual orientation revealing all that was necessary to know about a person. So shifting the endotic perspective from place to person means opening up the infinite, internally conflicted, shifting desires, ideals and interests of complex, human beings in the lifeworld. It means resisting the quantitative policing of one-dimensional clinical labels ('autistic') or social typing ('deviant') to restore the infinitely rich constellation of human experience and possibility. It is in this respect that the current vogue for 'transparency' is a form of blindness that is more to with the coercive narratives of macro-modernity (name and shame) than with any desire to account for the 'exquisite detail' of human fullness. Putting a figure on a number of articles published or on the amount of minutes spent in consultation may make the education or health service transparent to auditors but it makes them and the society that pays their inflated fees blind to the open-ended multi-dimensionality of genuine education and healthcare.

Implicit in the endotic understanding of humans, as we have noted, is the inevitability, the necessity indeed, of conflict. As Angélique del Rey and Miguel Benasayag have pointed out, part of the work of mourning for humanity is the acknowledgement that there will never be perpetual peace. Each time, they note, that there is a 'war to end all wars' which aims at bringing about the reign of everlasting peace, the scale of destruction and human suffering is greater than ever before (Benasayag and del Rey 2007: 56).This observation is crucial as an attention to the local, the micro, 'small' places, 'small' nations can lead to a kind of consensual smugness in the present or a censorious nostalgia with respect to the past when no false note was to be heard and everyone lived happily before in the green houses on the prairie. Local community does not entail an end to dissent. Much of the disappointed reaction of post 1968 activists was partly to do with an overly benign notion of community. Having overly idealized the small community they could not tolerate the inevitable and indeed desirable persistence of difference and conflict. The notion that having found the larger group difficult it is possible to retreat to the haven of your 'own' – peer group, buddies, family – and expect the comforts of uncomplicated, consensual intimacy, is to invite the counter-movement of disappointment. However, it is important to move the notion of conflict beyond the binary logic of specular confrontation where entities with fixed identities face up to each other in a zero sum of binary opposition. Conflict from an endotic viewpoint is not confrontation, it is conflict as engagement with the multidimensionality of human beings, their texts, languages and cultures. It resists the culturalist versions of contemporary biopower which in the name of avoiding a 'clash of civilisations' presents all conflict as confrontation through the binary stereotyping of Us and Them. The ultimate triumph of dictatorships as Miguel Benasayag and Angélique del Rey have pointed out is to present their opponents as pure adversaries (109). Confrontation in this scenario invariably leads to elimination.

An agonistic conception of human community in an era of micro-modernity, which runs directly counter to the beatific visions of universal understanding underlying many public pronouncements on the topic of globalization, takes as a basic premise the incomprehensibility of the other. That is to say, human interaction is not simply the revelation of what is already there. The reason is that in the movement to engage with the complex being of others, in the creation of some form of shared sense, some degree of commonality, the operation is not one of uncovering a universal substrate, waiting to be revealed in its pre-formed state, but the contingent construction of bottom-up commonality. It is useful in this context to invoke the distinction made by the Sinologist and philosopher, François Julien, between the Universal, the Uniform and the Common. For Julien, the Universal is the Universal of scientific reason, the claim, for example, that the atomic composition of water does not change wherever it is studied on the planet. Universal reason cannot suffer exceptions, there cannot be two hydrogen atoms in water in the United States and three in Australia, otherwise the claim is not universally valid. The uniform is a kind of perverse double of the universal, a phenomenon which has universal impact not because of the necessary implications of reason but because of a skilfully engineered ease of access. An example would be global fast food chains, the process of 'clonialism' we referred to earlier. When it comes to defining the Common, Julien characterises it as *fons* not *fundus*. What he means by this is that the Common is not what is left at the bottom (*fundus*) once everything has been taken away and all the differences have been removed but it is rather the source (*fons*) of what is potentially shareable through mutual intelligibility (Julien 2008: 213). A group can work out what it has in common, what are common interests and concerns but this work is processual. In other words, the working out is not the mechanical application of a predefined prescriptive agenda but the constructed emergence of shared ideals, preoccupations, values. The common, then, is best understood not from a building perspective as the ready implementation of a blueprint but as a form of what Tim Ingold would call 'weaving', the negotiated, imminent emergence of sense through inter-activity (Ingold 2000: 346). This sense of the constructed nature of the common is caught in Georges Braque's comment on the two nineteenth century landscape painters Émile Corot and Paul Trouillebert, 'The common is true. The similar is false. Trouillebert looks like Corot but they have nothing in common'. As becomes all too apparent when you travel abroad, being similar to someone (eg sharing the same nationality) does not mean that you necessarily have anything in common with them.

The danger, of course, is that the commonality which allows for communication across differences becomes the shared and exclusive property of the group who literally ex-*communicate* others. As stories of romantic love invariably show, the more intense the commonality, the more exclusive the affections. One of the functions of the universal has traditionally been to avoid excessively defensive local allegiances and to ensure that the potentially infinite capacity for inclusion of the common does not mutate into the actually infinite ability to exclude. But this critical universal must be understood in the context of human commonality not as some ahistorical, transcendent truth but as an incomplete and historically contingent operation, constantly subject to revision.

A necessary part of the acceptance of the internal multi-dimensionality of human beings is that in their mutual encounters it is different levels, different selves, different identities that will come into play at any given moment and alter the grounds and conditions of negotiated interaction. As William James once observed, 'A man has as many social selves as there are individuals who recognise him'. This feature obtains as much within as between communities. Admitting the necessity of the ontological dimension of conflict for the emergence of identity also involves accepting that there is no final, definitive reconciliation of opposites but that any arrangement is provisional, an unstable equilibrium, which does not rule out further conflict in the future. In short, it is this endotic understanding of conflict which can provide a way of thinking about contemporary multicultural societies in a manner that moves beyond revealed universalism and schismatic relativism.

This understanding of the multi-dimensionality of self also underscores the misleading nature of the 'one world myth' that Anthony Elliott and Charles Lemert refer to in *The New Individualism* (2006). This is the notion that the alleged contemporary 'crisis' in multiculturalism means that peoples should now return to the pre-migratory 'one world' of shared ethnic identity which was so cruelly disrupted by the advent of unassimilable newcomers. Not only does historical evidence discount the validity of this 'one world' ever existing for countless communities around the globe but the internal and external plurality of self and the constructed and negotiated nature of the common means that just as there are any numbers of potential and actual selves there are also (and have been) any number of potential and actual selves and worlds. Christopher Prendergast, drawing on the work of Victor Segalen, claimed that we 'are never "closer" to another culture (and hence liberated from the traps of ethnocentrism) than when we fail to understand it, when confronted with the points of blockage to interpretive mastery' (Prendergast: 2004: xi). The real failure to understand is the failure to understand that living subjects and their cultures are infinitely complex and indefinitely conflicted. In the next chapter we will consider how we might conceive of co-existence in local settings and how time once again crucially determines our arrangements.

Chapter Three

The World Turned Inside Out

The piper, it is said, calls the tune but in Ireland he is often expected, in addition, to explain it. The musician and folklore collector Séamus Ennis was no exception and he frequently prefaced his tunes with an account of their origin. One such tune was *Cornphíopa na Sióg* or the Fairies Hornpipe and Ennis's story went as follows. A man returning home from a wedding loses his way and 'if that happens to any of you, you have but to take off your coat and turn it inside-out and put it on again and you'll find your way home alright' (Ennis 2006). The wedding reveller does this and he ends up three fields away from his own house. At the bottom of the long field in which he finds himself there is a fairy host dancing to music played by a piper. Listening to the music he falls asleep and when he awakes next morning and goes home to tell people what he saw, no one believes him. It was only when they hear him play the tune he picked up from the fairies on the pipes that they decide he was not making it up. The tune was known ever afterwards as the 'Fairies Hornpipe'.

In a twinkling, the wedding guest is transported to the vicinity of his house. The vignette from Irish folklore anticipates the phenomenon of space-time compression in macro-modernity, to which we have already alluded, where successive generations find getting people and information from one point to another takes progressively less time. In Ennis's story, losing your way is also about finding your way but finding your way involves change, transformation, inversion ('you have but to take off your coat and turn it inside-out'). The coordinates in the musical parable are space and time. What happens when trying to find out where you are might involve turning your world upside

47

down before the sceptical welcome of homecoming? And how might the endotic perspective of micro-modernity and a politics of microspection re-enchant and transform the world in which we live?

The Czech novelist Milan Kundera in *Slowness* (1996) notes that when people want to remember, they slow down and when they want to forget, they speed up. He describes a man walking down the street:

> At a certain moment, he tries to recall something, but the recollection escapes him. Automatically he slows down. Meanwhile, a person who wants to forget a disagreeable incident he has just lived through starts unconsciously to speed up his pace, as if he were trying to distance himself from a thing too close to him in time. (Kundera 1996: 34)

For Kundera, place is bound up with pace. The more you seek to get away from a place, the faster you go. Conversely, the slower you go, the more you become aware of place, and more particularly, the more you become aware of the place of memory. Mnemosyne for the writer is the deity of deceleration. This is implicit in the notion of denizenship and durational time where occupation of a place over a period involves the recovery of previous memories, the kinds of memories celebrated by the organisation, Common Ground. One way of examining how we might reconsider a different notion of space and time is to look at how stories told about a particular place involve the manipulation of time and what the implications of those stories are for contemporary predicaments.

In order to provide a properly stereoscopic view of a place at a particular moment we will begin with two prose narratives, in two different languages, English and Irish Gaelic, both published in 2007 and both dealing with the lives of characters living in suburban Dublin. The novels are *The Gathering* by Booker prizewinner Anne Enright and *Cnoc na Lobhar* by Lorcán S. Ó Treasaigh.

In Enright's novel the death in England of a family member, Liam, brings the family together in Dublin for his funeral, a story narrated principally by his sister Veronica who is responsible for the repatriation of his body. The protagonist of Ó Treasaigh's work, Labhrás, is in an old folks' home awaiting in bitter recrimination the inevitable end stop of death. Death and old age bring with them their own rhythms. Both works, then, are studies in the effects of a change in tempo, memories bustling in as a fast-paced globalised Ireland is bracketed by grief and loss.

A common preoccupation for both Labhrás and Veronica is how to prevent a gathering in from becoming a falling out. That is to say, as they find time to think about the place in which they live and have lived, they are forced to think about the people who have shared that place with them, whether it be in the present or in the past. Labhrás, an old school nationalist, who has remained all his life deeply committed to the cause of the Irish language, sees his ideal of a shared place initially in expansive, communitarian terms. The Ireland that he has dreamed of is a collective enterprise:

> They shared life and language, sadness and happiness, joy and heartbreak, they stood side by side at baptisms and weddings, they supported each other from the cradle to the grave and you can be sure that if life did you a bad turn there would always be a helping hand to stop your fall. (Ó Treasaigh 2007: 68)[2]

'Muintir' – which might be approximated by the American English notion of 'folks' – is the term that is used by Labhrás to describe this cooperative community of equals who were united at an undetermined moment in the past by their common condition of being inhabitants of a particular place and remaining committed to the language of their forbears. As the story of Labhrás's life unfolds, however, the semantic range of the term contracts and Labhrás, up late drinking in the silence of his fractured household, contemplates his present with contempt:

> This is my house, this is my family and this is my life, I was thinking before I fell asleep on the couch and I dreaming of being somewhere else on the other side of the world instead of being on my own in my semi-detached garden, a citizen among the other semi-detached citizens, turning the earth for the sake of turning it until the day when I will descend into it, the black earth of my desire, the cold earth of the graveyard. (142)[3]

'Muintir' is no longer the extended family of an idealised past but the biological family of his living present. What is apparent in the narrative is that the space he has shared with members of his own family has become a place of intolerable strife as his ideological certainties inure him to a world that is changing and to personalities and values which are evolving. As time slackens, Labhrás begins in effect to take stock of the collapse of this imagined community of place and of the fallout of casting his own 'muintir' in the image of an Ireland that was not to be.

Anne Enright's heroine Veronica is similarly troubled by how families fail to live up to their own promise. Not only does she feel temporarily estranged from her own husband and children, but the experience of making the arrangements for Liam's burial makes her realise the extent to which her own experience of family growing up has always been deeply conflicted. Her own memories of relationships between parents and children in late modern Ireland on the eve of the economic boom are avowedly unromantic:

> Back in Belfield [campus of University College Dublin], my

best friend Deirdre Moloney had just been thrown out by her mother for nothing at all: a very low-key sort of girl, she only ever had sex twice. Children were being chucked out all over Dublin. All our parents were mad, in those days. There was something about just the smell of us growing up that drove them completely insane. (Enright 2007: 96)

The interest of these tales relate less to their specific settings in late modern Ireland but to the issues they raise as to how communities are to function in locales deeply implicated in global socio-economic relations.

Progeneration

To see how this might be the case it is worth examining briefly the distinction the social anthropologist Tim Ingold makes between 'genealogy' and 'relation'. In the genealogical model, individuals are seen as entering the lifeworld with a set of ready-made attributes which they have received from their predecessors. The essential parts which go to make up a person, his or her culture, are handed on, more or less fully formed. The popular image for this conception of personhood and community is that someone has something in their 'blood' or more recently, 'in their genes.' The relational model, on the other hand, relates to the concept of 'progeneration' which Ingold defines as the, 'continual unfolding of an entire field of relationships within which different beings emerge with their particular forms, capacities and dispositions' (Ingold 2000: 142). That is to say, whereas the genealogical model is concerned with past histories of relationship, with the unfolding development of a bundle of preset attributes in a given space, the progenerative model is primarily concerned with current sets and fields of relationships for persons in a given lifeworld.

The genealogical model has obvious affinities with the notion of 'family' or indeed, muintir, in both a narrow nuclear and wider kinship definition of the notion. It is the model which clearly informed the 2004 Citizenship referendum in Ireland that introduced the notion of bloodline into definitions of Irish citizenship. It is also a model which is implicit in the blueprint for future economic development of the country promoted by the social commentator David McWilliams. In his work *The Generation Game* based on a TV series of the same name, he argued that Ireland's hopes lay with its large overseas diaspora, who are seen to have a more viable emotional and cultural commitment to the island's future than recent non-diasporic migrants to Ireland (McWilliams 2008). In the genealogical model the descent line is separate from the life line and life and growth become the realization of potentials that are already in place. So being Irish is to be a member of a family which through immediate (domestic) or extended (diasporic) bloodline is endowed with a culture that is determined by essence rather than context.

One consequence of the model is that cultural difference in Ireland, as in many other countries, is almost invariably construed as 'diversity'. That is to say, the notion of diversity, which is becoming something of a mantra of beatific official pronouncements on our multicultural world, supposes different groups possessed of different sets of ready-made attributes. These are juxtaposed in the shop windows of different contemporary states and each group acting out their pre-defined cultural script contribute to the effervescent display of cultural diversity. So the invocation of diversity which is often seen as a way of countering nativist genealogical exclusiveness in fact tends to partake of the same logic but simply multiplies the examples of genealogical inheritances rather than challenges the basic logic.

In the narratives of Enright and Ó Treasaigh, this logic is questioned, albeit in less than explicit ways. Labhrás finds sympathy and self-understanding of a kind through his imaginary conversations with Darach, a refugee in time from the ravages of the Black Death in 14th century Ireland. Darach comes not only from a different age but he is outside of Labhrás's family circle. He is an antecedent not an ancestor. Similarly, Veronica's movement beyond the emotional stalemate of her life is not through the fraught communion with her immediate family but by way of the encounters she has with relative strangers in Ireland and in England. Stephen Dedalus's befriending of Leopold Bloom or Marcel's coming of age in the company of the *invertis* in *La Recherche* are earlier paradigms of a way of viewing personhood and community which is progenerative rather than genealogical. In other words, it is the sets of relationships which individuals and communities enter into at a given moment which engender change and the emergence of new forms, forms which are not obsessively pre-scripted by birthright. From this perspective - and this is crucial when we acknowledge the conflicted complexity of place - it is more appropriate to speak of positionality rather than diversity. Positionality, in effect, is to do with the sets of relationships obtaining at any moment between and within groups, relationships that are subject to an endless process of change, change which is the very stuff of the human life-line and which crucially includes the dimension of power. Adopting a progenerative as opposed to a genealogical stance obviates the danger of localism shading into parochialism. Small is beautiful in some eyes because a reduction in scale makes exclusion a more viable option, an exclusion legitimised by the genealogical border posts of bloodlines. Maintaining the open-ended, fractal dynamic of micro-modernity, on the other hand, involves a commitment to the progenerative model of human interaction. But even if the writers are suggesting that relation-ships need to be construed differently and that the cultural homeliness of the genealogical is no longer viable where are these relationships going to take place and how will place itself affect them in a globalised world? How is shared place going to affect the forms that positionality will take as the society evolves through time?

Altericide

It is something of a philosophical and sociological truism (which does not make it any the less true) that our identity is defined through others. Just as difference is inconceivable without distinctness, so too identity is unimaginable without someone or something against which that identity is contrasted (Julien 2008: 34). Ireland as a country, for example, had notably defined itself through its relationship to Faith (religion), Fatherland (nationalism) and *Fataí* (potatoes (Gael.) = synonym for land). An intense sensitivity to the view and perceptions of others has been a notable feature of Irish public life and the lavish domestic coverage of the then Irish Premier Bertie Ahearne's address to the US Congress, as opposed to the general indifference of the US media, showed how the good opinion of powerful others has been an intrinsic component of Irish self-identity. Part of the difficulty in late modern Ireland was that the Others which defined the country, namely, ethnic conflict (nationalism), a confessional state (religion) and an agricultural economy (land) were no longer dominant as ways of defining emerging Irish identities given that political, social and economic developments in the nineties and noughties spelled an end to Irish exceptionalism (Cronin 2008: 175-185). But the changing status of otherness in one specific locale needs to be situated in a wider context to get a keener sense of the dilemmas faced by populations trying to make sense of where they stand in the present global moment.

Dominique Quessada has argued in *Court traité d'altéricide* [A Short Treatise on Altericide] that the most striking feature of the contemporary age is the prevalence of what he calls 'altericide' which he defines as the 'systematic liquidation of the modes of existence delineating the figure of the Other' (Quessada 2007: 40).[4] Quessada traces a history for altericide which begins, he argues, with the Christian Incarnation. When a deity takes on a human form, there is a diminution in the radical otherness of the divinity. As Yahweh, the radically unknowable Other, becomes Christ, the mortal human, the gods not only mingle with mortals. God becomes mortal. Jesus as man becomes the subject of readily identifiable human narratives in the gospels. Following through to the present, Quessada sees the collapse of Soviet communism and the worldwide embrace of the market economy as a further evidence of the demise of the Other, as the alternative economic and geopolitical order of the Soviet bloc gives way to the hegemony of commodity capitalism. The very concept of global-isation itself with its notion of the 'global' as all-inclusive is symptomatic of the absence of an exteriority, of an outflanking of critique by larger categories of co-option. The death of the Other does not mean, however, that there are no longer any differences. On the contrary, there have never been so many. As Quessada intimates:

> If differences can proliferate, it is because the Other is no longer there as an overall obstacle. The metaphysical concept of the Other is what contained (in the dual sense of encom-passing and holding back-preventing-restraining) differences because it represented the absolute difference compared to which the differences and micro-differences which co-exist today did not have the slightest bit of meaning. (Quessada, 63)[5]

A direct consequence of the destruction of alterity is the multipli-cation of differences. It is not because the Other disappears that we are all condemned to sameness. It is possible to find the summary analysis of Quessada too glib, and to point to a flour-ishing contempt for others in global Islamophobia, resurgent anti-semitism and virulent anti-immigrant rhetoric in Europe and elsewhere. However, it is nonetheless striking that the collapse of the public sphere in Ireland and elsewhere over the last decade is partly attributable to a specific form of altericide. In Ireland, all the potential sources of political opposition in the form of unions, community groups and NGOs were brought into partnership arrangements with government and so-called 'social partnership' signaled the end of any serious opposition to official policy in the wider society. Similarly, the support of all four of the major political parties on the right and left for a Yes vote in the Irish Lisbon referendum or the broad political front backing guarantees for the banking sector in October 2008 showed that any sense of radical otherness had succumbed to the managerial consensualism of a professionalized political class. That this phenomenon does not somehow announce the end of difference is borne out by the hugely successful pop sociology of social commentators who engage in the endless differentiation of the pollster and marketeer: Yummy Mummies; GI Janes; Hibernian Cosmopolitans and so on (see McWilliams 2005). The differences can be parsed endlessly because they no longer make any difference.

How then does altericide affect contemporary perceptions of place and more specifically, how does globalization inflect this perception in particular ways? A classic trope of Hegelian thinking is the master-slave dialectic, a recurrent figure in Hegelian descriptions of human interactions. Quessada evokes in the late modern world the existential figure of the *Esclavemaître* or SlaveMaster, 'a slave who is at the same time a master while remaining a slave, a figure in whom the distinctions of master and slave become literally indistinguishable, without the two states ever really being confused with one another' (Quessada 2007 : 126).[6] This collapse of categories, the emergence of this seemingly contradictory, hybrid figure that is the Slavemaster is singluarly revealing of a deep uncertainty about what it means to inhabit a place in the early 21st century. In 2007, Maureen Gaffney, an Irish psychologist and media pundit, offered the Master's narrative in a warm encomium to the feelgood factor of the transient period of Irish affluence in the early 2000's:

> We seemed to have used our prosperity as an opportunity to enjoy stable family relationships, to develop our personal expressiveness and to show the world what we're good at. Given Ireland's economic, cultural and religious history – still in living memory – we have embraced prosperity, the good life and personal freedoms with unabashed relish, and we won't lightly let them go. (Gaffney 2007)

The tone is not untypical of a slew of articles and public pronouncements in the boom years which presented Ireland as moving beyond the depressed divisiveness of the eighties to the irenic utopia of the 21st century. In contrast to the discourse of the Irish as Masters and Mistresses of all they surveyed was an equally explicit narrative of dystopian malcontent. In this view, Irish society was one where citizens were the slaves of a brutalizing and alienating system that led to the abandonment of values that had previously sustained it. The most notable exponent was the Ombudsman and Information Commissioner Emily O'Reilly who in an address to a conference held in 2004 claimed:

> Many of us if we have any developed sensibility recoil at the vulgar festival that is much of modern Ireland, the rampant, unrestrained drunkenness, the brutal, random violence that infects the smallest of our townlands and villages, the incontinent use of foul language with no thought to place or company, the obscene parading of obscene wealth, the debasement of our civic life, the growing disdain of the wealthy towards the poor, the fracturing of our community life, the God like status given to celebrities all too often replaced somewhere down the line with a venomous desire to attack and destroy those who were on pedestals the week

before, the creation of 'reality' TV, more destructive in its cynical filleting of the worth and wonder of the human soul than anything George Orwell could have imagined. (O'Reilly 2004)

O'Reilly and Gaffney co-exist in the same society and both would presumably see themselves as describing the same country. What is less important than adjudicating the respective merits of the Master and Slave narratives here is to suggest that public receptivity to both of these radically different interpretations of a particular time and place is in part to do with the presence of the SlaveMaster as a dominant paradigm in a liberal-democratic market economy. On the one hand, the denizen is consumer, the supreme master of choice, the active agent of destiny, the flattered subject of his or her multiplying desires. On the other, the denizen as producer is simply another object to be used, an eminently replaceable part of a process, a figure on a balance sheet, utterly subject to forces over which he or she has no control (Laval 2007: 15). Hence, the repeated feeling that the denizen is both master and slave depending on which role he or she happens to occupy at any given moment. The overall emergent effect is that of the SlaveMaster, the shifting, uncertain inhabitant of the contemporary moment, whose view of place is alternatively that of subject or object, in control or out of control, at home in the world or trying to cope with the world at home.

One factor that the denizen as SlaveMaster has to contend with is the incidence of time and how the accelerated time-space compression of globalization impacts on appropriations and re-appropriations of place. The writer and cartographer Tim Robinson in his work *Stones of Aran: Laybrinth* speaks of the daughter of one of his native informants on an island off the west coast of Ireland, Inismore, 'I imagine his daughter is one of the smart young women I see driving into Cill Rónáin as if they were on a freeway to a shopping mall, slamming themselves through the island's spaces; she runs a chilly, hygienic, tourist-board-approved b&b [bed and breakfast], and hardly tolerates her father in the back kitchen' (Robinson 1995: 18) The elderly man and the young daughter may inhabit the same geographical space but their time zones are markedly different. The daughter's car slams through spaces collapsed by the acceleration of time. Robinson, for his part, sets himself the task of walking each of the many thousands of fields which cover the island. What Robinson attempts to do in his work is to restore the infinite complexity of those spaces through a process of endotic travel, partly by his own decelerated practice of walking the fields of Inismore but partly also through the memories of older inhabitants, his informants, whose physical slowing down becomes a creative act of remembering. In a sense, Robinson's move is linked to the rehabilitation of dwelling as a creative or enabling way of engaging with places subject to the peripheralising dismissal of velocity, a foregrounding of denizenship where 'caring for local places and contexts' is powerfully determined by an ability to shift time zones. Implicit in the move is a relationship to land and place which is not wholly overdetermined by an obsession with ownership. That is to say, a cult of place does not always make for a culture of living. Finbarr Bradley and James Kennelly have noted, for example, that possession and care are not necessarily common bedfellows. They claim, 'In Ireland, ironically, a lack of concern with design and aesthetic quality tends to go hand in hand with a preoccupation with place. This affinity with place (it can hardly be called a sense of place) appears to have little to do with tending, cultivating or enhancing the material environment' (Bradley and Kennelly 2008: 49). In the light of Ireland's demonstrably poor environmental record (McGee and O'Brien 2008), a seeming allegiance to place, repeatedly articulated in advertising campaigns around community involvement in local sporting organisations, is accompanied by a manifest inability or unwillingness to care for it. The hold of property over the national psyche in many countries as evidenced by the almost neurotic rehearsal of anxieties and fears during the post-crisis downturn stands in vivid contrast to the general lack of urgency and engagement in addressing the systematic deterioration of place through climate change. In effect, what joins the concerns of Robinson to the ruminations of Enright's Veronica or Ó Treasaigh's Lahbrás is how to dwell properly in a place. How is it possible, for example, to dwell meaningfully in places which have altered so dramatically in such a relatively short period of time?

Time

Quessada claims that one further consequence of the phenomenon of altericide is the triumph of the spatial over the temporal. That is to say, the preferred time of democracy is the present as both the past (different political regimes) and the future (everything from popular revolt to terrorism) both potentially threaten its legitimacy. He argues:

> The absence of time, specific to the movement of democracy towards its realisation, means that, to be and to take place, everything must be and take place at the same time, that is to say, in the same space. (Quessada 2007: 100)[7]

Arguments take time. It takes time to put forward sequentially a thesis, a counter-thesis and eventually some form of synthesis. In the soundbite instantaneity of media-saturated democracies, the time of exposition is anathema. This is not say that different viewpoints are not aired. They are, if only because there is a legislative obligation on state broadcasters to do so. But to return to our earlier discussion of genealogy what is offered is the spectacle of diversity rather than an engagement with positionality. In other words, different opinions on a budget, for example, are summarily aired, opinions coming from politicians to trade unions to employers' bodies. The opinions are simply juxtaposed as if they were all equally valid and everyone had the same ability to determine outcomes in the society which is patently not the case, as evidenced by strikingly uneven distributions of income in Irish society (Nolan and Maître 2007: 27-42) and across the planet. So there is diversity of a kind but rather less understanding. The time needed to tease out strands of power and influence is denied in favour of the spatialised collage of clips, individuals and groups rehearsing the pre-scripts of the representational ('on behalf of my party I would like to say'). In a sense, space is what happens to place when time tends towards zero. The less time a person has to dwell on what it means to live in a particular place, the more the place they inhabit becomes filled with the spatialised ubiquity of commodity advertising, ratings-driven media product and context-less information bites. Place becomes the site of the multiple surfaces of consumption, a tantalizingly fragmented space, detached from any longer-term sense of what it means to dwell in and be responsible for a particular place and how the place might be positioned relative to others. In this context, there is nothing more conservative than the repeated exhortations to abandon the past and move rapidly into the kinetic utopia of the future. A genuinely radical scenario involves abandoning the obsessive-compulsive rigidities of the short-term for the unsettling and innovative dwelling perspectives of the long-term.

In the short term, of course, there is nothing more difficult than planning for the long term, for what Stewart Brand has called the 'Long Now' (Brand 2000). The acceleration of technological change, the short-horizon perspective of a market-driven economy, the next-election perspective of representative democracy and the frantic multi-tasking that has become the daily lot of so many living and working on the planet mean that a potentially fatal short-sightedness becomes the norm.

It is often said that what a people strive for is the greatest happiness of the greatest number but it is worth bearing in mind that the greatest number have not yet been born. Therefore, when we speak about the greatest good, what we really mean is the longest good. There is not much we can do to improve the quality of life of those who are already dead on this planet but immeasurable good can be done to improve the quality of lives of those who will be born or come to live on it. In order to give force to this notion of the longest good, it is necessary to make the taking of long-term responsibility a core concern of a politics of microspection. How might we do this and what are the short-term implications of long-term thinking?

Writing in an Irish newspaper the environmental specialist Frank Convery argued that 'a sustainable climate change strategy for Ireland must focus on the long term' (Convery 2007). His immediate concern was Ireland but his remarks could have been addressed to decision makers in any country on the globe. The Stern Report and the reports from the UN Intergovernmental Panel on Climate Change have clearly spelt out the consequences of global warming and unchecked carbon emissions for water availability, sea levels, species survival, agriculture, ocean acidification, coral reefs, weather patterns and human settlement. The repeated conclusion is that humanity must begin to act now if it is to avoid catastrophic consequences in the long term. So farming practices, the types of crops produced, the way cities are planned and transport systems organised, the kinds of goods and services produced and how they might be produced must change in the short term if there is to be a viable long-term future for humans and many other species on the planet. However, in the era of the instant opinion poll, the relentless style barometers of 'What's Hot' and 'What's Cold' and the instantaneous e-mail message, how are denizens to escape the tyranny of the moment?

In the language of the Tewa Indians of the American Southwest there is an expression, 'pin peyeh obe' which translates as 'look to the mountain'. When the Tewa elders use the phrase they mean that if we look at things as if from the top of a mountain we get a broader view, we see what lies ahead (Brand 2000: 144). We also, however, if we turn in another direction, see what lies behind. In other words, the long view is not only forwards but backwards. Just as our present was once someone's distant future, if we want to make sense of what might or ought to happen in the future we need to understand how we got here from our distant past. As our sense of time extends in both directions being responsible for what might happen to future generations involves being equally responsible for learning appropriately from past generations. To think far back is to develop the reflex of the long view which is not the subsidised indulgence of the scholar but a core survival value of any culture which wants to exist into the future.

The impending ecological crisis points to the overwhelming need for society to stand back, take stock and adopt the long view if the many places that go to make up the planet are to have a sustainable future. To do this it is necessary to analyse how having been turned 'inside out' by changing relationships of time and space affects in very profound ways the human capacity to dwell in any given place. But crises are famously moments of opportunity and it is perhaps time to call a different tune for the piper, a tune that is about place rather than property, about denizens rather than citizens and about the far-seeing rather than the short-sighted. What that tune might be is the concern of the next Chapter.

Chapter Four

Microspection

The present moment is one of decision. The discrediting of the international financial system through the fallout of the subprimes crisis and the incontrovertible evidence of the implications of climate change means that global communities have to act now to ensure a viable future for the planet's six billion inhabitants. A Green agenda without a robust sense of social justice is doomed to irrelevance. Cosmetic ecology with a sense of business as usual clearly addresses neither the problems of the planet nor the needs of society. By ending social inequality, particularly destructive and wasteful forms of production and consumption can be halted. Presiding over continued growth in inequality is the most effective break on bringing about the changes in values and practices which are central to a properly eco-centric conception of economy and society. Economic growth in forms that have been practised until now are clearly no longer possible. The need is to imagine forms of growth based on a wholly different understanding of the relationship between human beings and their planet. Tomorrow is too late. We must clearly act today if there is to be a tomorrow.

In formulating alternative forms of politics it is important to recognise what has manifestly failed. It has to be honestly acknowledged, for example, that certain forms of political transformation, not only on the right (neo-liberalism) but on the left (statist communism) have had calamitous consequences. There is nothing progressive about a politics which is scripted in advance by the social and political movements of the past, as if the world stopped changing, say, at a given moment in October 1917. A truly radical politics is just that, a politics which may borrow from the past but is not a hostage to it, and more importantly, is a politics which engages with the unpredictability of the present in unpredictable and challenging ways.

The politics of microspection outlined in this Chapter has two fundamental components, the analytic and the operational. Analytic microspection is the proper investigation of places and their inhabitants through methods and practices which reveal the full, fractal complexity of human habitation. The activities of seeing and revealing are fundamental here. Operational microspection is the application of forms of social, economic and political organisation to local places in a way that ensures their future sustainability. The vision of economy and society underlying a politics of microspection is one of the basic unit of sustainability being the local in a transnational context. As Alastair McIntosh has observed, 'It is only if we can find fulfilment in close proximity to one another and local place that we can hope to stop sucking what we need from all over the world' (McIntosh 2008: 71-2) The local as is made apparent through analytic microspection is not cut off from but open to the world. There is a continuous dialogue between in here and out there. For a society to survive it must engage in forms of wealth creation which are sustainable and to this end we argue for forms of economic activity which draw on and give sustenance to local place. In outlining what might constitute the elements of a politics of microspection, both in its analytic and operational dimension, the aim is not to be exhaustive, an impossible task in an extended essay of this kind, but to offer examples of what such a politics might look like in practice.

Analytic microspection

Adelard of Bath, an eminent English scholar and Arabist of the 12th century, dedicated his influential *On the Use of the Astrolabe* to Prince Henry, the future Henry II. In his introduction, Adelard, uses a homely image to justify his love of the new learning to the young prince:

> You say that whoever dwells in a house is not worthy of its shelter if he is ignorant of its material and makeup, quantity and quality, position and peculiarity. Thus if one who was born and raised in the palace of the world should forbear after the age of discretion to know the reason for so marvellous a beauty, he is unworthy of it and, were it possible, ought to be cast out. (cited in Lyons 2009: 128-29)

Adelard's challenge to the young nobleman was to embrace the new scientific understanding of the world which was creating considerable disquiet in Church circles due to its challenge to clerical authority and its Arab provenance. But more broadly, Adelard's concern for a proper understanding of the 'palace of the world' has lost none of its relevance eight centuries later. The question that is increasingly being asked is to what extent we are worthy of the shelter of the house that is planet earth, if we are 'ignorant of its material and makeup, quantity and quality, position and peculiarity'? Overcoming this ignorance requires us to be attentive to the manner and form of our attentiveness.

In a paper published in 1977, the French mathematician Benoît Mandelbrot asked the following question, 'How Long is the Coast of Britain?' The answer was that at one level the coast was infinitely long. An observer from a satellite would make one guess that would be shorter than say, a travel writer like Paul Theroux in *The Kingdom by the Sea* (1984) negotiating every inlet, bay and cove on the British coast and Theroux's guess would be shorter than that of a tiny insect having to negotiate every pebble (Mandelbrot 1977). In other words, as James Gleick notes, 'Mandelbrot found that as the scale of measurement becomes smaller, the measured length of a coastline rises without limit, bays and peninsulas revealing ever smaller subbays and subpeninsualas at least down to atomic scales' (Gleick 1987: 96).

What Mandelbrot discovered was that the coastline had a charac-
teristic degree of roughness or irregularity and that degree
remained constant across different scales. Mandelbrot named the
new geometry that he had originated fractal geometry. The
shapes or fractals in this new geometry allowed infinite length to
be contained in finite space. The analogy with endotic travel
described in Chapter One is compelling and examples abound in
accounts of travel of the overwhelming detail of the particular. In
her exploration of the Irish coastline, Rosita Boland describes a
scene on Sherkin Island, off the southern Irish coast, where she is
looking for the whereabouts of an American friend, George
Packer. She meets an elderly woman who tells her that Packer
lives a long way past the church and that the woman herself has
not been past the church in years. Sherkin Island is three miles
wide:

> Hadn't been further than the church for years? A house on the
> next hill was a long way away? Continuing on towards the
> house, I thought again about distances and how, within the
> three-mile area of Sherkin, there was a space so open and
> densely-textured that two lives need never entangle and at
> the same time, a space so physically small that a couple of
> hours tramp and you could say you had "seen" the island.
> (Boland 1992: 216)

The shift in scale is a revelation for Boland. Small is not simple.
The complexity of the open and 'densely-textured' space is the
roughness or irregularity or complexity that carries across scales.
A casual remark by an elderly islander uncovers the infinite
possibility of travel in the finite space of an island. As we saw
earlier Tim Robinson's exploration of the fourteen thousand
fields of Árainn, the largest of the three Aran Islands, is called,
appropriately enough, *Labyrinth*. The fractal dimension of travel
leads Paul Theroux to the inescapable conclusion that 'every mile

of England was different' (Theroux 1984: 29).

So what analytic microspection involves primarily is taking a closer look at our immediate surroundings. But what is to be gained by this keener attention to what surrounds us and is there a risk of the emergence of a hyper-parochialism, of a resentful hunkering down in the backyard of local or regional identity? If we first examine what the gains might be it should be possible to address the very real concerns contained in the second part of the question.

Charles Forsdick in a work on French travel literature in the twentieth century noted that the perceived decline of diversity was one of the most common preoccupations of the literature. Travellers go to far-off places, tell their readers that the 'exotic' is an illusion, that everywhere has now become much the same and the writers themselves are the last witnesses of differences which are about to disappear forever:

> The implicit sense of erosion [of diversity] that characterizes certain nineteenth-century and earlier twentieth-century attitudes to the distinctiveness of individual cultures may, in its more extreme manifestations, have bordered on apocalypticism; but the transfer from generation to generation of such renewed prophecies of entropic decline uncovers the pervasive and conservative tendency according to which transformation is cast as death and loss. (Forsdick 2005: 3)

Forsdick draws a comparison with Raymond Williams' analysis of the trope of the decline of rural England which Williams saw less as a precise event happening at a specific moment in time than as a 'structure of feeling' running through English writing for centuries (16). Each generation of writers in England from the seventeenth century onwards lamented the fact that the countryside they knew had now disappeared forever. As the same countryside could not logically keep on repeatedly disappearing, the critic concluded that the laments were less a matter of absolute empirical truth and more to do with a particular way of viewing the natural world. In other words, though the notion of the decline of diversity may be differently accented depending on whether the context is the triumph of the Fordist factory or the predatory designs of globalizing Goliaths, there is a sense in which the theme of the imminent demise of diversity is akin to a recurrent structure of feeling as proposed by Williams (Williams 1979: 156-65).

Things are always getting worse and the cultural critic like the despairing travel writer can only report on a world that is about to lose its distinctiveness and leave us adrift in a 'standardized world.' Chris Bongie discussing the terminal pessimism of Claude Lévi-Strauss's *Tristes Tropiques* on the future of diversity observes:

> Dire visions such as these however, most often resemble each other not only in their pessimism but also in their propensity for deferring the very thing that is being affirmed: although humanity is settling into a "monoculture", it is at the same time still only *in the process of*, or *on the point* of, producing a "beat-like" mass society. (Bongie 1991: 4, his emphasis)

There is no time like the present to tell us about all that is soon to be past. The attraction of the entropic, of course, is that it does away with the historic. Indeed, Thomas Richards sees the scientific origins of the concept of entropy as a convenient means of ensuring the end of history, 'As a myth of knowledge, entropy, like evolution, would seem to place history outside the domain of human activity. Because it transfers agency from human beings to physical principles, it ostensibly represents a pessimistic relinquishing of all possibilities of social control' (Richards 1993: 103). A sense of hopeless resignation in the face of entropic inevitability leads not surprisingly to a pervasive feeling of disenchantment. The world gets smaller and smaller, everywhere is similar, all High Streets look alike, McDonalds and Coca-Cola become the plague rats of global sameness, infecting sites of difference with the bacterium of homogeneity. As the world shrinks, our hopes diminish. It is this worldview which is directly challenged by a politics of microspection. In its analytic mode, it involves a deep, rigorously close attention to a world which is captivating and everywhere unique in its endless, fractal complexity. The re-enchantment is as much about seeing what is actually there as it is in discovering the continuously expanding world of fractal or endotic enquiry. Implicit in the approach is not only a riposte to the discourse of exhaustion, the planet as McWorld, but microspection frees the local from the dangers of reductive typicality. That is to say, one of the common responses to the phenomenon of globalization is the assertion of difference. A key feature of international tourism, for example, is the theming of specific locations where distinctive local forms of music (reggae, Irish traditional), dance (highland jigs), drink (German beer), architecture (painted gable ends in the Austrian Tyrol) become an important selling point for the local 'product' on the global market. The specificity of place is reduced to a semiotic shorthand that can be easily recognised and profitably replicated (the Irish Pub). In short, in the commodified versions of the local there is a denial of the multi-dimensionality of place and their inhabitants that is revealed through microspection. For this reason, there is nothing inherently progressive or liberatory about the championing of the local or the particular or the specific if the local or particular in question is understood as static rather than dynamic, as one-dimensional rather than multi-dimensional. Accent, for example, can be a ready guide to embedded complexity of place, where differences of class and cultural capital are carefully folded into the sounds of the local language. A humorous example is offered by the popular writer Paul Howard in his description of the changing names of the light railway, the DART (Dublin Area Rapid Transit), as it moves through the city of Dublin:

> Those intrepid souls who are prepared to stay on for the entire hour-long journey, running the risk of being robbed at knifepoint, will notice the way the name of the service changes according to the local dialects. In the well-off North Dublin suburbs of Howth, Sutton and Bayside, it's known as 'the Dort'. As it passes through Kilbarrack, Killester and Harmonstown on its way to the City Centre, it becomes 'de Deert'. When it crosses the Liffey, skirting the coast of Dublin 4, the vowel sound becomes softer again and it sounds more like 'the Doort'. Through Glenageary, Dalkey and Killiney, it becomes 'the Doorsh'. When it reaches Shankill, it's "de fooken traying", and by the time it reaches Bray, it's just something people throw stones at. (O'Carroll-Kelly 2008: 67-68)

Naming and pronunciation are reminders of real differences, of the multiple dimensions to a locale which are irreducible to the seductive and marketable shorthand of typicality. The local is distinctive but microspection suggests that it is endlessly and tantalizingly distinctive. The French Carribean writers Jean Bernabé, Patrick Chamoiseau and Raphaël Confiant in a wholly different context argue for the necessary specificity of Francophone Caribbean writing and culture bringing into play the notion of 'diversalité' or diversality:

> Creole literature will have little time for the Universal, that is to say, this hidden alignment to western values[...]this exploration of our specificity[...]brings us closer to the world itself[...]and opposes universality with the opportunities of a world which is diffracted but reassembled, the conscious harmonization of the diversities which have been maintained:

Diversality. (Bernabé, Chamoiseau and Confiant 1989: 41)[8]

Implicit in the notion of 'diversality', as opposed to 'universality', is the idea that though the Caribbean may be made up of 'small' islands, the imaginative territory and the linguistic potential of the region is of a wholly different order. When they write that, 'our world, however small, is vast in our minds' ['notre monde, aussi petit soit-il, est vaste dans notre esprit'], they are foregrounding the fractal complexity of places of human dwelling that cannot be reduced to the packaged stereotypes of resort tourism (Sheller 2003). But are these worlds, however 'vast' for some, in effect too small for others? If countless numbers have fled small-town bigotry, isolationism, conformism, is there not a good reason for this, is there not a sense in which the local can only offer a way in but never a way out?

To rethink this question in our contemporary age it is necessary to consider the implications of informationalism that we alluded to in Chapter One. One of the effects of the rise of the network society is that the notion of who is our neighbour gets redefined by the communications technology at our disposal. We may have more regular contact through the internet with a friend on the other end of the city or the other side of the globe than with our physical neighbour in the apartment or house next door. This means in turn that if your neigbour wants to get in touch with someone on the other end of the city or the other side of the planet, he or she is only one degree of separation away from that person, namely you. The world becomes at once smaller and bigger for your neighbour. The mathematicians Duncan Watts and Steven Strogatz in their study of how small worlds come into being drew on their work in network theory. Starting from a circle of nodes where each node is connected to its immediate and next-nearest neighbours, they added a few extra links connecting randomly selected nodes. These long-range links offer the crucial short cuts between distant nodes and so dramatically shorten the average separation between all nodes. As Albert –László Barabási observed:

> The surprising finding of Watts and Strogatz is that *even a few* extra links are sufficient to drastically decrease the separation between the nodes. These few links will not significantly change the clustering coefficient. Yet thanks to the long bridges they form, often connecting nodes on the opposite side of the circle, the separation between all nodes spectacularly collapses. (Barabási 2003: 53, his emphasis)

In human terms, the relative short number of degrees of separation which will allow me to contact anyone in the world (between three and six degrees or intervening persons) is based on 'the fact that a few people have friends and relatives that do not live next door any longer. These distant links offer us short paths to people in very remote areas of the world. Huge networks do not need to be full of random links to display small world features. A few such links will do the job' (53).

The default model adopted by Watts and Strogatz is one that closely resembles the circumstances of many human beings in that it presupposes a close, inner circle or 'cluster' of relatives or friends. As we saw with the geographers Geraldine Pratt and Susan Hanson in Chapter Two, 'most people live intensely local lives' (Pratt and Hanson 1994: 10-11). However, the implication of the 'small world' theories developed by Watt, Strogatz and others is not that small is suffocatingly beautiful but surprisingly open. It takes a relatively small number of links to produce a remarkable degree of connectedness. But this connectedness is only made available of course if we are aware of the existence of the distant links. The Swiss writer Nicolas Bouvier tells of being on a small island off the coast of Ireland and being pressed by his host, a small farmer and fisherman, about life in the big cities of the United States. He is several weeks into his visit when he realizes that the farmer/fisherman had spent over two decades working in New York city. His host had in effect mischievously disguised his own status as a 'distant link' to the New World (Bouvier 1990).

This is precisely the task of analytic microspection, the bringing to the fore of the multiple connectedness of local communities, the revelation of those distant links which connect individuals and communities in one locality to people and places in many different localities around the world. Analytic microspection, in a sense, ensures a reduction in those degrees of separation that make other parts of the world seem remote or irrelevant. Conversely, the absence of a politics of microspection means that the distant links, the long bridges, are not assumed to be there to ensure the connectivity that permits the 'small orbit' in one place to be brought closer to small orbits elsewhere. In this scenario, the small world of the tightly clustered leaves no room for the Small World of the distantly related.

A further dimension of network theory which has implications for the ways that we think about a politics of microspection is the importance of what the sociologist Mark Granovetter has called 'weak ties' (Granovetter 1973: 1360-1380). On the basis of his research, Granovetter established that when it comes to finding a job, launching a new fashion, letting people know about a new restaurant, weak social ties are much more important than close friendships. So, in the words of Barabási:

> Weak ties often play a crucial role in our ability to communicate with the outside world. Often our close friends can offer us little help in finding a job. They move in the same circles we do and are inevitably exposed to the same information. To get new information, we have to activate our weak ties[...]The weak ties, or acquaintances, are our bridge to the outside world, since by frequenting different places, they obtain their information from different sources than our

immediate friends. (Barabási 2003: 43)

If our close friends have access to much the same sources of information as ourselves then it stands to reason that new sources are more likely to come from those who move in somewhat different circles than our own. Bearing in mind then the importance of 'weak ties' for innovation and connectivity, the detailed attention that is paid to the communities immediately surrounding us becomes all the more crucial. In other words, one of the less helpful notions of local community is one that we described in Chapter Three as 'genealogical' where the local becomes the site of People like Us, preferably Blood Brothers and Sisters. Strong bonds in this framework take primacy over weak ties. However, what endotic or fractal forms of viewing involve is showing precisely how the weak ties of the progenerative provide the distant links that are denied by the clustering instincts of blood groups or the ethnic fantasies of belligerent self-sufficiency. The baleful economic, political and scientific effects of the expulsion and or destruction of the Jewish population in the second millennium of European history is tragic testimony to what happens when members of a local community are suddenly removed and their classification as 'weak ties' (religious aliens) or 'distant links' (the conspiracy of World Jewry) makes the world a dangerously small place indeed. Filling in and making populations aware of the full historical, social, cultural, and economic detail of places has the very real potential to highlight the centrality of progenerative notions of community to the human vitality and sustainability of place. The work of analytic microspection serves not to dis-connect people from place ('we don't know who we are anymore') but rather to re-connect inhabitants to real as opposed to strategically fabricated histories of place. In this way, places becomes sites of progenerative potential as opposed to genealogical commemoration, dynamic fora for change rather than static enclosures of attrition. What looking closely at the present and past of what immediately surrounds us involves, among other things, is a commitment to dwelling knowingly in a specific place. Separation from what has gone to make up and what informs a place, the desire to objectively possess rather than subjectively dwell, leads almost inevitably, to separation from the full range of people who inhabit a particular locale. Not only does separation from the world around us lead to well-documented ecological harm but it narrows empathy to an imagined community of other possessors, united by the attributes of hereditary entitlement. Looking again rather than looking away is the necessary precondition of transformative vision. How ways of seeing things differently can inform ways of doing things differently will be considered in a brief exploration of the operational dimension to a politics of microspection.

Operational microspection

If architecture is about anything, one could say that it is about dwelling, about the philosophy and science of dwelling in a particular place. Pierre Thibault in his manifesto for a 'Slow Architecture' (www.pthibault.com) argues that the primary concern of architecture in an era of ecological crisis should be with the creation of added value in the long term. For Thibault, this entails the creation of urban structures where dwellings are near services, schools and workplace. Local, vernacular traditions often provide a guide to forms of sustainable dwelling which integrate the specific characteristics of place while minimising harmful effects on the immediate environment. He takes as an example, the houses built in rural Quebec in the 19th century. Designed facing southwards, they were built with as few openings as possible in a northerly direction and built using stones and timber found in the immediate vicinity by carpenters and masons working in the local neighbourhood. A stove placed in the centre of the house catered for the essential human needs of heat and nourishment (cooking). The judicious use of resources and minimal use of energy in a vernacular architecture in perfect osmosis with the surrounding territory showed what was possible in earlier periods. More contemporary architectural projects such as those of Luis Barragán in Mexico, Sverre Fehn in Norway, Asplund in Sweden or Dominic Stevens in Ireland show what is possible when local traditions are linked to contemporary building techniques to develop forms of dwelling that integrate and interact with the local in a framework of long-term sustainability. As Thibault notes:

> In the case of each building, the architects find themselves concentrating on a particular place, exploring it, trying to know its history, understanding its potentialities, its properties, the habits of the those who live there, community life. An active contemplation allows for a better understanding of all of this. (Thibault 2009: 115)[9]

Living anywhere is only possible, of course, if it is possible to make a living. If it desirable to live near a workplace, what kind of workplace is it possible to envisage that respects the integrity of local relationships, that allows human to become denizens in the their professional lives and engage in ecologically sustainable economic practices?

There are many potential responses to this question but a key element in a political economy of microspection is the so-called Social Economy. The Social Economy includes cooperatives, mutual societies, non-profit associations, foundations and social enterprises. What distinguishes enterprises in the social economy is that their primary aim is not capital accumulation. That is to say that they generally seek to make a profit in order to ensure the stability and durability of the enterprise but the accumulation of capital to generate income for shareholders is not their primary purpose for existing. In terms of management and ownership, the fundamental principle is one person, one vote not one share, one vote. This means that those who work for enterprises in the social economy have a direct say in and control over how the business is run. In France, for example, in producers' co-operatives, 51% of the capital and 65% of the voting rights are held by workers. The core values of enterprises in the social economy are equitable distribution of wealth, solidarity, shared values, accountable management, personal growth, voluntary membership, freedom from State control and personal growth (de Kerorguen 2009: 8). Entities in the social economy can range from a group of village farmers who set up a co-operative to market their produce to a group of savers who set up a mutual fund to ensure that they receive an adequate pension. It is estimated that at present approximately 10% of all European businesses are social enterprises, with over 11 million paid employees or 6% of the working population of the European Union (European Commission 2009). Social enterprises are to be found in almost all the sectors of the economy, such as banking, insurance, agriculture, craft, various commercial services, health and social services and so on. Worldwide, it is estimated that there are about 750,000 cooperatives, with a combined membership of 775 million and employing 100 million workers (de Kerorguen 2009: 9). The potential for job creation is illustrated by the workers cooperative movement in Spain (*sociedades laborales*) which in the space of a few short years has created 17,000 enterprises employing 100,000 people. Implicit in the model of the social economy is that workers have a significant degree of control over their immediate working environment and that it is the collective interests of the producers of wealth that take precedence over the financial self-interest of transnational shareholders whose primary concern is short-term (monetary) returns not long-term ecological sustainability. As the worldwide economic crisis at the end of the first decade of the twenty-first century revealed, the model of financial capitalism underlying the neo-liberal credo of economic development since the late 1970s had led to spectacular levels of inequalities in terms of remuneration, an alarming lack of control over the activities of senior management, ecologically catastrophic forms of growth and devastation with respect to the human fallout of unprincipled delocalisation. Taking charge then of the local workplace, reinvesting places of work with a sense of responsibility, real power (as opposed to the corporate fiction of 'empowerment') and a long-term concern with added value shows how structures of ownership, management and accountability as articulated through the social economy illustrate the socio-economic working out of a politics of microspection. Making profits a means not an end, transferring control to those who actually generate wealth and making markets work for people and not vice-versa means first and foremost looking to where people find themselves so that through their work they can contribute to the betterment of the places where they live while contributing to more sustainable forms of development and a more equitable distribution of wealth. Central to this movement, however, is democratic control. The limits to initiatives in the area of 'corporate social responsibility' or the various forms of 'nice capitalism' favoured by conservative social commentators who admit, however reluctantly, that something needs to be done about the planet is that the photo-op of charity is substituted for the transformative work of real change. Encouraging young people to set up Youth Banks so as to establish a process of providing grants to local youth led projects may win your bank a prize and a night out in dinner jacket to collect a President's Award from local luminaries but it does nothing to change the fundamental relationships of power and control that ultimately determine the quality of life in local working and living environments. There are options beyond the predatory practices of shareholder-led capitalism and authoritarian State communism (the parody of workers' rights in China) and it is a core element of a politics of microspection to advance these options as part of genuinely emancipatory economic practices. The choice of the word 'politics' is deliberate. Changes in power and changes in control involve a politicized conception of the economy. Leaving issues of profound ecological, economic and social change to the vacillating goodwill of the well-heeled condemns humanity to a form of eco-charity that is as uninformed as it is disabling. Any serious and sustained ecological change demands radical and inescapable changes in the current, dominant models of political economy.

An important motivating factor in the emergence of the concept of the social economy is the need to deal with the ecological consequences of reckless productivism, whether practised by liberal-democratic market economies or authoritarian communist regimes. Part of the response to this concern is Serge Latouche's formulation of what he calls the 8Rs as the pre-conditions for the move to a more sustainable life on earth, 'Re-evaluate, reconceptualize, restructure, relocalize, reduce, reuse, recycle' (cited in Dupin 2009: 21). As demonstrated by a number of contemporary initiatives, a large number of these 'Rs' can in fact be reduced to one, relocalize.

The 'Transition' idea first emerged in Kinsale, Ireland in 2005 and has since spread to a number of countries worldwide, with a significant presence in the United Kingdom. The basic concept is that a local community of interested individuals in a particular place (village, island, city) come together and explore how to address the challenges of peak oil and climate change. A community defined Energy Descent Action Plan is put together and the Plan is implemented over a 15 to 20 year timescale. In addition to aiming at a sharp reduction in carbon emissions, Transition initiatives restore the resilience communities have lost as a result of over-dependence on cheap oil. The ability to resist significant ecological shocks (resilience) is crucially situated at local level and Transition initiatives are primarily local in their orientation. The types of initiatives are grouped under the following headings and are worth citing *in extenso* to make apparent how initiatives take shape at the micro-level:

- Food: People source a lot more of their food from local producers, often organic. They increasingly share produce grown in their gardens and allotments and some new community gardens. They have well organised deliveries from local farms and farmers' markets. There are a growing number of newly-established Community Supported Agriculture schemes, and peri-urban market gardens. A few are experimenting with pig and chicken clubs, and community bakeries are starting to mill local flour. Some people are cooking prepared meals for time-pressed neighbours. Many people are learning to cook and garden for the first time, with Transition groups offering training and reskilling in both.
- Transport: Fuel for personal car use has become much more expensive than before, so Transition groups' Transport theme groups have organised ride share schemes, collection and delivery systems for children, shoppers and social events. Living without a car is now possible in a way that it was not before. Car share schemes mean that people have access to borrowed or hired larger vehicles when they need them. There is a lot more cycling among the fit and healthy, and the high price of fuel has meant that many businesses now encourage people to work from home where possible.
- Household Energy: Transition initiatives have, with funding from their local authorities, initiated 'insulation clubs', where people have learned the best ways of reducing household heating needs and help each other do it. Numerous tricks and tips to use less energy have become popular. A growing number of Transition initiatives have now set up Energy Services Companies (ESCOs), owned by the community, to

provide locally generated electricity through community-owned wind, solar, hydro and biomass schemes.

- Re-use, recycling, repair: Many local schemes have been started to extend the life of clothes, repair goods and appliances, creating some part-time employment. Workshops in making do and repairing are commonplace, often inviting older people to share their undervalued skills with younger generations. Much of the local food is distributed in re-usable containers. Transition initiatives are facilitating the bulk-buying of goods designed for durability and which can be repaired when needed.

- Local economy: People have begun to do a lot of organised trading and exchange with each other, sometimes for money, sometimes for local currency, but very often as favours. They give and receive goods that they no longer want, help each other with childcare, rides, deliveries, and many other services. Groups of young people offer 'technical support' on anything from computers to DVDs. This enables people's money to go much further, and provides some income for those without jobs. They have identified the like-minded local independent businesses and artisans whom they preferentially patronise, and give them ratings and recommendations on their websites (Hopkins and Lipman 2009: 10-12).

The Global Ecovillage Network which is present in around forty countries around the world is similarly concerned with the development of ecologically sustainable and economically viable lifestyles at local level. Network members include large networks like Sarvodaya (11,000 sustainable villages in Sri Lanka); EcoYoff and Colufifa (350 villages in Senegal); the Ladakh project on the Tibetian plateau; ecotowns like Auroville in South India, the Federation of Damanhur in Italy and Nimbin in Australia; small rural ecovillages like Gaia Asociación in Argentina and Huehuecoyotl, Mexico; urban rejuvenation projects like Los

Angeles EcoVillage and Christiania in Copenhagen; perma-culture design sites such as Crystal Waters, Australia, Cochabamba, Bolivia and Barus, Brazil; and educational centres such as Findhorn in Scotland, the Centre for Alternative Technology in Wales and Earthlands in Massachusetts in the United States (http://gen.ecovillage.org).

Implicit in both the Transition and Global Ecovillage Network is the shift from *externalisation* to *internalisation*. Paul Virilio, for example, chronicling changes in contemporary experiences of time and space notes, 'the importance now attached by firms to the EXTERNALIZATION of their production – including research and development – at the expense of their former specific local base. So, for several years now, the *external* has become more important everywhere than the *internal* and geophysical history, is turned inside out, like a glove!' (his emphasis) (Virilio 2009: 19).[10] A graphic illustration of the practice of externalization is the purchase by Daewood Logistics of 1.3 million hectares of arable land on the island of Madagascar. The purpose is to provide a secure food source for the population of South Korea but 70% of the island's population currently live below the poverty level (66). What is more, the island has been identified by the biologist and zoologist Edward Wilson as one of the planet's twenty-five 'biodiversity hotspots'. These hotspots only cover 1.4% of the earth's surface but account for 43.8% of all known plant types and 35.6% of species of mammals, birds, reptiles and amphibians living on earth (Wilson 2002). Externalization of course is a core feature of the post-Fordist economy and the very term 'globalization' indicates the global reach of the external where the British working class are now said to live in China (source of so many manufactured goods) and where what the Indian scholar Harish Trivedi has termed 'cybercoolies' in low-cost call centres service wealthy customer bases in advanced industrial nations (Trivedi 2004). In a sense, forms of externalization have been in evidence ever since

David Ricardo formulated his theory of comparative advantage where industrialised nations import agricultural produce from nations that enjoy the comparative advantage of still possessing fertile land for the production of food (Ricardo 2004). These nations in turn buy manufactured goods with earnings from the sale of foodstuffs and begin their own process of industrialisation.

The difficulty is that the form of intensive food production and population growth that exhausts the soils of industrialised nations eventually affects those nations enjoying a comparative advantage in the realm of agriculture and they too face the problem of finite natural resources. The limits to externalization are evident in what we now know about human impact on terrestrial ecosystems. Between 40% and 50% of the earth's surface has been modified by human activity, the concentration of carbon dioxide in the earth's atmosphere has increased by around 30% since the beginning of the industrial revolution, half of the world's water reserves are used by human beings, in recent history a quarter of the world's species of birds have been wiped out and two thirds of the world's fish species are currently fully or over exploited (Vitousek, Mooney, Lubchenco, Melillo 1997: 494-499; Millennium Ecosystem Assessment 2005).

The turn to the local, the internal, as demonstrated by the activities of the Transition and Global Ecovillage Networks and as articulated by the politics of microspection, suggests that after the revolution of externalization which marked the era of macromodernity (the global managerial and distributive possibilities of time-space compression) the next revolution will be a revolution of internalization. In other words, the way transport, industry, architecture, agriculture, energy, finance is organized, will have to radically reverse the compulsive externalization of the globalized market economy and move to practices of internal self-reliance and resilience. Many of these practices as described above are already being implemented. It is important, however, that in describing a future revolution of internalization that we be clear about what the implications are for a progressive worldview.

In the kinetic euphoria that accompanies contemporary eulogies to the global, the dizzying rate of global exchange is often equated to the relentless onward march of liberal democracy and the advent of a world marketplace of ceaseless cultural exchange (Friedman 2006). The defensive local allegiance of the particular has no place in the fraternal embrace of the universal. Enlightened supra-national governance or the inclusive joys of global citizenship are the termini of the accelerated voyage away from the retrograde claims of the specific. Universal love for all peoples and all species represents a kind of radical externalization of sentiment which envelops the planet in a outward burst of fellow feeling. However, are internal repudiation and external celebration the only grounds for intelligent sympathy or due care?

The philosopher and critic Val Plumwood has expressed a useful scepticism with respect to the viability of sympathies which are too indiscriminate in their focus:

> ...this "transpersonal" identification is so indiscriminate and intent on denying particular meanings, it cannot allow for the deep and highly particularistic attachment to place that has motivated both the passion of many modern conservationists and the love of many indigenous peoples for their land. (Plumwood 1994: 152)

Plumwood argues that, in fact, it is internalization not externalization which becomes the effective basis for a meaningful engagement with struggles and issues elsewhere:

> Care and responsibility for particular animals, trees, and rivers that are known well, loved and appropriately

connected to the self are an important basis for acquiring a wider, more generalized concern. (145-6)

It is in fact the local connection, the ready identification of a particular animal, tree, river, predatory oil company or abusive state practice in a local setting which makes possible the ethical imagining of the importance of species preservation or social justice in other proximate, micro-sites. In this sense, internalization becomes a highly effective form of mobilization in starting from concrete, near to hand examples to address issues that have a resonance beyond a specific locale. The movement inwards is an opening up, not a shutting down. As Alastair McIntosh has observed, 'I must start where I stand. As children, we used to be told that if you dug a really deep hole, you'd come out in Australia. I think in some ways this is very true. If any of us dig deep enough where we stand, we will find ourselves connected to all parts of the world' (McIntosh 2002: 7).

The presence or absence of a connection to other parts of the world is often presented as a co-efficient of the acceleration of time. That is to say, the quicker a link can be established with a place on the other side of the planet, the closer it becomes. Acceleration then becomes a cardinal virtue, bringing us all closer together, hastening the advent of truly global proximity. Acceleration is not, however, simply the forward movement of an abstract altruistic impulse. It has had very real and significant consequences for humanity. One of the puzzles which preoccupied economists for a long time was why although the world's population had exploded in the space of two centuries, living standards did not plummet everywhere as predicted by Malthus among others. From 1820 onwards, global population figures began to rise significantly, but the average standard of living doubled between 1820 and 1900, doubled again between 1900 and 1950 and trebled in the years between 1950 and 2000. So although the world's population between 1820 and 2000 has increased by approximately five billion average global living standards have risen equally dramatically (Fitoussi and Laurent 2008: 24). Davis Gregory Clark has shown that if the direst Malthusian predictions did not come to pass it was due to improvements in the quality of labour which allowed to the same tasks to be done more effectively and this coupled with the acceleration in technical progress during the industrial revolution meant that though population rose in 18th century England average living standards rose rather than fell. The annual average growth rate in technical advances was well below 0.05% before 1800, about one-thirtieth of current levels (Clark 2007). In another domain, the emergence of network-based economies where informatics and telecommunications networks were able to offset the disadvantage of geographical location, comparative advantage became increasingly a matter of temporal advantage. Getting services to the customer (a translation, a new design, a set of accounts) more quickly would, all other things being equal (quality, competitive pricing and so on), be the decisive factor in awarding the contract or the commission. Hence, the eagerness of the nation states and supra-national institutions like the European Union to invest in universal broadband. In addition, the returns on acceleration have long bewitched financial markets. After the collapse of the financial system in 2008-2009, a number of analysts were perplexed as to how hedge funds and large banks such as Goldman Sachs were able to continue making very large sums of money. It turned out that an important contributory factor was the use of high-frequency trading. Powerful computers allow traders to transmit millions of orders at lightning speed, subtly manipulating share prices and in the process earning billions of dollars at the expense of less technically savvy conventional or ordinary investors (Duhigg 2009). The effectiveness of the system is based on the fact that certain marketplaces, like Nasdaq, allow traders to peek at orders for 30 milliseconds – 0.03 seconds – before they are shown to everyone else. Traders can then make a quick profit by very quickly trading shares that they know will be in high demand. What is eloquent in the example is not the existence of a potential loophole in market practices or the scope for abuse but the centrality of speed to the turbo-capitalism of a global market economy. Indeed, the scale and rapidity of the collapse of the financial markets and the suddenness of the onset of recession in many economies worldwide at the end of the first decade of the new century (Iceland) showed how speed was a reversible value and could trigger spectacular forms of collapse alongside dramatic forms of growth.

We saw in Chapter Three how forms of deceleration and ways of remembering are closely linked. Slowing down allows the forgetful to be reminded of truths that are not always palatable. Paul Virilio, who has long had an interest in the effects of the speed revolution, points to one of these inconvenient truths:

In 1977, I wrote that speed meant the aging of the world. Thirty years on, the argument has been proved right, because of the huge impact of GLOBAL MOBILIZATION on the political economy of the wealth of nations who up until now had treated with disdain this principle of acceleration which nevertheless called into question the history of technical progress incompatible with the quantitative reserves necessary for the survival of nations. (Virilio 2009: 40)[11]

The finitude of resources is one factor that obviously complicates the utopian promise of endless acceleration. Whereas in earlier human history it was humans who sensed their finality faced with the uncontrollable force of nature, it is now nature whose finality is being dictated by uncontrollable forms of accelerated growth. Another outcome of increased rates of change is the direct effects not only on resources and stocks but on climate as context for human activity. Greenhouse gas emissions have risen by 70% between 1970 and 2004 and the concentrations of carbon dioxide in the atmosphere has increased continuously throughout the period. If global warming is to be limited to between 2 and 2.4 degrees Celsius overall reductions in emissions of between 50% and 85% will be necessary by the middle of the century with respect to levels in 1990. Apart from the quantitative and contextual breaks on the kinetic promise of ceaseless acceleration what are the less obvious consequences of the reign of speed for an operational politics of microspection? The consequences can be loosely grouped under three headings, though they are all, as we shall see, inter-related. These headings are ground, time and identity.

Ground

During the height of the economic boom in Ireland the sliding doors in the Arrivals area were decorated with a fresco of opulence. But the opulence was not located in Ireland. It was externalized. It was to be found in Dubai where very large cars and very tall towers were presented as the incontrovertible signs of a shiny future available to owners of well-provisioned Irish (or foreign) bank accounts. The location of the large advertising mural in an airport was not accidental. Airports are all about mobility, transition, acceleration. They are where people come and go. An index, indeed, of how globalized countries are is the volume of their air traffic. Airports are physically grounded somewhere but they are implicitly about not being on the ground but being up in the air: passengers go to airports to take leave of the ground and being 'grounded' by security delays, strikes, company collapse, is such a bleak scenario that it usually makes national, primetime news. The tall towers, too, carry a promise of elevation. Suspended in the air, the owners of the penthouses, can survey the ground far below, before winging through the skies to another preferential tax haven in the heavens. For Virilio, the endpoint of what he calls the political economy of speed is the triumph of *meteopolitics* over geopolitics. The exhaustion of the earth's resources (underground), the exponential increase in gated communities in urban centres and suburban areas (ground) and global concerns about the climate (overground) means that the 'sky is now more important than the ground' (Virilio 2009: 58-59).[12] The cult of mobility, the economic premium of speed, and the diminution of responsibility which comes with rapidity of displacement (transnational corporations leaving locals to clean up the ecological mess they leave behind) does indeed make being in the sky as opposed to being stuck on the ground a more attractive proposition for global elites. But, of course, it is not only elites who are on the move but many millions of workers who leave a particular place (ground) to go elsewhere in search of a better life. What is a privilege for elites can, of course, be a form of tyranny for migrant labour forces where they are left 'hanging in the air' uncertain about their status, citizenship rights and long-term future.

Emphasising the importance of specific, local places and the rights and responsibilities of denizenship or dwelling in these places does involve re-asserting the primacy of the geopolitical over the meteopolitical. But is not the championing of place, of ground, *sol*, not dangerously reminiscent of blood and soil ideologies of the twentieth century? Is there not something inherently reactionary about movements that are hostile to movement? To consider how these questions might be answered it is necessary to return to a notion which was discussed in Chapter III, the notion of time, but on this occasion, in the context of economic practice.

Time

One way to conceive of an economy is as a closed system, as a mechanism, with different constituent parts whose positions can be marked and whose evolution can be predicted with the appropriate mathematical tools. Looking at economies as basically about prices and quantities, prices determining the quantities available for supply or purchase on the market, has a conceptual manageability which is attractive to the formal, quantitative bias of particular forms of computing. The notion of the self-regulation of the market implies that all the information necessary to the smooth running of market mechanisms is basically contained within the system of pricing. The free inter-action of the constituent parts will allow the system to reach equilibrium, serving the optimal interests of the parts in question. No outside interference (e.g. government) allows for maximal inside effectiveness. Variations of this paradigm have become firmly implanted in the minds of policymakers and media commentators at the expense of a more dynamic conception of what is involved in an economic system. Jean-Paul Fitoussi and Éloi Laurent take the example of the difference between two types of watches to illustrate the difference between mechanical and dynamic systems and by extension the impor-tance of time itself in the economy.

In older, mechanical watches it was perfectly possible to take apart the watch and then re-assemble the watch and have it working again. The mechanism was in a sense perfectly self-contained. In battery-driven watches, on the other hand, no matter how expertly the watch is put back together again, nothing will happen if the battery is spent. The watch is not wholly self-contained. It is a dynamic system, dependent for its functioning on an element which is external to it, a battery. What is more, the element that the watch is dependent on, a battery, is a finite resource, linked to the energy reserves of the planet. In essence, then, to conceive of the economy as a political economy is to conceive of it as a dynamic system which is not only open to the influence of political decisions over, for example, the distrib-ution of resources, but is also involved in continuous interaction with social and physical processes. Most importantly, from the perspective of a progressive re-grounding of politics, implicit in the notion of the economy as a dynamic system is the recognition that time is not only an integral part of economic systems but that the effects of time are often irreversible. The economy is not a mechanism running autonomously where the question of time and the direction of its flow is a matter of indifference. What the depletion of the resources of the planet and the anthropogenic causes of climate change clearly indicate is the irreversible effects of human activity which are both caused by and in turn feed into economic practices. As Fitoussi and Laurent argue, there is a clear entropic dimension to the relationship between the world's economies and the existence of finite resources (Fitoussi and Laurent 2008: 52-54). In a sense, what happens when the entropic dimension comes to the fore is that we become more aware of the 'thickness' of time that we referred to in Chapter Two. The amnesia of speed, the heady acceleration of development, where the geographical past is forgotten and the terrestrial future ignored, becomes more and more difficult to sustain as the sky pilots of post-modernity are increasingly grounded by the entropic restrictions of a depleted planet.

There is a further and different sense in which time has thickened for economic and political thinking and this is related to our earlier discussion of the notion of the Long Now. Hans Jonas in *The Imperative of Responsibility* (1984) discusses the respective vulnerability of nature and vulnerability of humanity and claims we become aware of the vulnerability of nature when it is human existence itself that is being threatened by the imminent destruction of the environment. However, not only does this environmental finitude point to the irreversibility of certain forms of human economic activity but it places the question of responsibility in a time-frame which extends way beyond the present. A planet properly cared for should be able to sustain human life for many millions of years barring an unforeseen external catastrophe, such as a meteorite collision. A failure to act responsibly and become, wittingly or unwittingly, complicit in the destruction of the planet as a viable home for humanity is not only to place in jeopardy the lives of the billions of people already living on the planet but the lives of the many billions who have not yet been born. The difficulty for the unborn, as Jonas points out, is that they cannot speak from the future; they are dependent on advocates in the present. Therefore, there is no escaping the long-term consequences of short-term decisions but envisaging these long-term consequences involves factoring into the immediate present a notion of durational time which is deeply inimical to current versions of society and the economy which discount the centrality of a different order of time. Not recognising the longer time-frame is tantamount to a form of suicide, the accelerated forgetfulness of a humanity heading for the fatal smash that will truly be the movement to end all movement.

As we saw in Chapter Three when the lives of fictional characters begin to slow down, they become aware of what is going on around them. However, it is not only what is actually going around them but what has already gone on around them. Labhrás enters into dialogue with a character from 14th century Ireland and the narrator of *The Gathering* brings the reader back to the lives of her grandparents. Time begins to extend in all directions. As time thickens, the perception of place sharpens and of how that place has come to be. What happens to the characters as the tales unfold is that they grow in knowledge. They come to know more about themselves and the people and places around them, even if that knowledge is rarely certain and always provisional. This link between deceleration and knowledge is crucial and it is a link which will point to the inseparability of analytic and operational microspection when it comes to a progressive politics of re-grounding.

An important function of knowledge is that it too constitutes a form of irreversibility. It is usually difficult (though not impossible, as in the case of neurosis) not to know something once you know it, however unwelcome that knowledge might be. What is more there is often a multiplier effect in that knowledge generates in turn more knowledge so that if it cost \$19,500 to process one million standard calculations in 1890 in OECD countries, improved knowledge of computing meant that in 2000 it cost \$0.00000007729 (Fitoussi and Laurent 2008: 53). Knowledge typically involves the discovery of the unknown, the unsuspected, and the new. In this respect, knowledge has obvious anti-entropic or negentropic properties. It increases the sum of what we know and is an additive rather than subtractive operation. So the question that might be asked then is how do we deploy the anti-entropic qualities of knowledge to positive effect and counter the fatal irreversibility of environmental destruction?

One answer to this question is to re-ground knowledge in types of practices which are linked to the exercise of denizenship. That is to say, forms of knowledge can be advocated and explored which deepen and complexify a sense of place in order to ensure not only its flourishing in the present but its viability into the future. These are the forms of knowledge outlined in our discussion of analytic microspection and they potentially and actually inform the practices related to transition initiatives and the social economy. Integral to the transmission of these forms of knowledge is the type of educational system that acts as a carrier. Ivan Illich in the 1960s had already initiated a trenchant critique of an educational system that cut children off from the world around them. The kind of knowledge offered by formal education, he argued, was too often of a disembodied kind so that what children learned in the classroom brought them further away from rather than closer to the world or worlds they inhabited. In addition, the rich learning environments that surrounded the children (launderettes, cafeterias, service stations, cinemas) were wholly ignored as potential sources of educational insights (Illich 1995). More recently, and in a less explicitly urban vein, Alasdair McIntosh has argued for a genuinely 'elemental' education at elementary level, 'They [children] need contact with nature where they can learn about matter and energy, cosmology, the atmosphere and its weather, the soils and the rocks, and the rivers, lakes and seas and their flora and fauna' (McIntosh 2008: 240). If education acts a bridge between the analytic and the operational it is important to bear in mind that knowledge is not only of the kind that can reconnect us to the world that is around us or that can provide techno-scientific solutions to ecological problems or conceive of regulatory frameworks to limit the catastrophic environmental fallout of dominant industrial practices. There is also what we know and need to know about the irreversible consequences of decoupling growth from social justice.

As we noted earlier in the discussion of the Long Now present-day policymaking must acknowledge the consequences of decisions for the lives of many millions of human beings that have not yet been born. However, it is difficult to envisage any sense of vertical equality (inter-generational) if there is no existing sense of horizontal equality (intra-generational). That is to say, as was observed in Chapter Two with respect to regional poverty and income inequality in Central and Eastern Europe, a startling increase in inequalities within societies has been a marked feature of economic growth across the planet in recent decades. If there is a marked reluctance to aim for equitably distributed benefits of growth in the present (horizontal equality) it is difficult to see how equitable forms of growth are going to be pursued for the benefit of future generations (vertical equality). The major difficulty with horizontal inequality is that the world's real population problem is rich people. The planet cannot afford the number of rich people whose claim on the world's resources is far in excess of their numerical importance. If there is no balance struck in the present between availability of resources and fairness of distribution, no genuine commitment to social justice, then there is no reason to be believe the situation will be any different in the future. Indeed, if it was, it would be too late. It is inequalities in the present not in the future which will decide whether the planet has in fact a future. In addition, as Laurent and Fitoussi point out, in societies with advanced levels of inequality, it is difficult for a significant proportion of the population to give any thought to the future. They are simply too preoccupied with the all-consuming task of day-to-day survival (Fitoussi and Laurent 2008: 67).

Essential to the emergence of a society with due respect for social justice and ecological sustainability is the ability of people to participate in political activity without fear of intimidation or persecution. It is perfectly possible, for example, for a market economy to function in the absence of fundamental human rights and it is unapologetically authoritarian regimes such as China which have registered spectacular levels of economic growth as adjudged by the conventional barometers of GNP and GDP.

On the other hand, in 2007 China became the world's leading emitter of greenhouse gases and over 30% of China's waterways are deemed to be seriously polluted (Organisation for Economic Co-Operation and Development 2007). The liberalization of markets provides no ready guarantee for the advent or flourishing of democracy but political freedoms are indispensable to ensure the vitality and effectiveness of community responses to the environmental threats at local level, the level at which global damage begins. If people are not allowed to organize, act and represent themselves in their localities, they are powerless to prevent ecological carnage. Just as ecological sustainability is inseparable from social justice, it cannot be considered in isolation from political freedom.

David Garland in *The Culture of Control: Crime and Social Order in Contemporary Society* notes about many modern societies in recent decades that, 'there has been a marked shift of emphasis from the welfare to the penal modality[...]The penal mode, as well as becoming more prominent, has become more punitive, more expressive, more security-minded[...]The welfare mode as well as becoming more muted, has become more conditional, more offence-centred, more risk conscious' (Garland 2001: 175). Greatly expanded periods of detention for questioning, the ubiquitous spread of CCTV cameras, data retention, electronic surveillance, and the continuous growth in private security firms are an increasingly common feature of life in democratic societies with the insidious banalisation of 'counter-terrorism' measures in the everyday life of the community. In the context of the present essay, I want to consider one aspect of this 'penal modality' which is bound with the way the relationship between identity and place gets re-defined in an age of acceleration.

In Chapter Three, we noted Milan Kundera's observation that the faster we go, the more we forget. This forgetting can in itself be liberating, if the past is felt to be unhelpful or burdensome. Hence the almost mythical association of speed with freedom, and the feeling of Getting Away from It All, preferably as fast as possible. But there is a worrying paradox in this association which is highlighted by Paul Virilio when he observes that, 'each time the speed of movement increases, so too do control and traceability' (Virilio 2009: 20).[13] Biometric passports, ubiquitous video surveillance, electronic tagging, continuous transfer and stocking of passenger data point to the fact that as movement accelerates so does the pace of panoptic control. Knowing where someone lives, their fixed or spatial 'identity', becomes much less important than knowing where they are going or have gone, their temporal identity or 'traceability'. So the promise of liberation promised by acceleration turns to out be the open prison of ever more intrusive surveillance.

Resisting the erosion of civic liberties, the relentless spread of coercive institutional paranoia, brings us to an aspect of the politics of microspection that may initially seem contrary to its mode of operation. In the language that is often used to describe education, we talk about the ability of education to 'enlighten' or 'reveal' or 'illuminate'. Part of the defence of a politics of microspection from an analytic standpoint is precisely it would seem this ability to clarify or bring into the light what had previously been obscured or concealed. The all pervasive logic of evaluation and assessment in every area of public life from education to audience ratings would appear to conform to that most desirable of ethical goods, transparency. How could a progressive politics possibly entertain the idea of the obscure or the shadowy or the opaque in the light of well-documented histories of corruption in many regimes, both democratic and non-democratic, and the long struggle of progressive political movements to hold the powerful accountable for their wrong-doing? To try and answer this question it may be worth trying to answer another. What is the definition of a free society? For the philosopher and psychoanalyst, Jean-Claude Milner, it is a society that protects the materially weakest from the strongest in the society. He goes on to add:

> The true friend of freedom holds to one conviction; leaving aside the fairytales where the weak become strong (revolutionary dream), for effective freedom, in the last resort there is only one material guarantee, necessary, even if not sufficient – the right to privacy, guaranteed to the weakest with respect to the strongest. (Milner 2005: 14-15)[14]

In the popular understanding of liberal democracy, the individual is the basic building block, the ultimate source of strength but, as Milner argues, every group and institution whether family, school, private enterprise or public body wants to grab hold of the individual, making him or her, 'the geometric site of weakness.' That is to say, the only force at the disposal of the individual to resist the complete colonization of his or her inner life is a degree of impenetrability. The current doxa of assessment, key performance indicators (KPIs), transparency, accountability driven by the confusion of the ontological and the economic (if you can't put a price on it, it does not exist) relates in essence to a nineteenth-century dream of a government of things replacing a community of subjects. In other words, whether envisaged by right-wing scientist technocrats or left-wing historical materialists, the basic notion is that the miserable and uncertain decisions of human beings be replaced by scientific laws which would determine and regulate the political, economic and social interactions between humans. For this to become practicable, it is necessary to move from formal equality (everyone enjoys the same rights) to substantial equality (everyone is substantially the same). Thus, human beings are not treated as the multi-dimensional speaking subjects we described in Chapter Two, incommensurable and separately unique but rather the aim is to introduce a regimen of radical pseudo-equality where anyone can be substituted indifferently for anyone else. You do not need to know anyone or anything intimately to be able to evaluate, all you need to know are the numbers. How much does she earn? How many articles did he publish? How long did she spend with that patient? This regimen of commensurability is the equality of things, so many interchangeable grains of sand. So one finds, for example, in Marxist movements, the recurrent tension between movements of liberation, based on the aspirations and actions of groups of incommensurable subjects, and forms of historical materialism in thrall to the government of things. Milner, not surprisingly, sees Stalin as a grim embodiment of the latter, 'Doubtless, fully aware of what he [Stalin] was doing, he chose to turn everything into things: politics, people, history, Stalin himself. The absolute reign of things, he called death. He affirmed this in the end, death alone wins out' (23).[15]

Underlying the all-pervasive cult of evaluation and the tyranny of the quantitative is a culture of death. A striking example of this is the media popularity of various forms of evidence-based medicine, in particular, those relating to forensic medicine. The ideal forum for the display of expertise in a culture of evaluation is the autopsy. *Air Crash Investigation, Forensic Detectives, Deep Sea Detectives, Decoding the Past,* and many other similar programmes, draw on forensic medicine as the ultimate arbiter of truth. Death brings its own certainties. The messy, living subject becomes the malleable, dead object and evidence becomes the language of things, the messages from beyond the grave. Knowledge that is not 'expertise', that does not speak the quantitative language of lifeless objects, that does not turn open and uncertain subjects into closed and certain objects, does not count in the rigor mortis of evaluation.

An avowed aim of a politics of microspection must be to champion a culture of life against a cult of death. This is not only in the sense of the struggle to preserve life on the planet but also in demonstrating through the fractal, endotic immensity of the lives of human subjects - their radical incommensurability – the necessity of forms of democratic co-existence that are based on tough trust rather than rigid control, respect for subjects rather than indifference to objects and a notion of identity that is open-ended and multiple rather than one-dimensional and confining. Implicit in microspection as outlined in this essay is that there is properly no end to what we can know about a place or the beings (human and non-human) that dwell there. Hence, degrees of impenetrability are not only inevitable but desirable insofar as they both acknowledge and safeguard the freedom of human subjects to grow in self-knowledge and change through time. As we noted in Chapter Two, in the context of the writings of Victor Segalen, it is not knowing everything which feeds a desire to know. If there is no impenetrability, on the other hand, there is nothing left to know. We are left with the dead inner landscape of the subject who has been thoroughly data-mined. The Nazi propaganda minister, Goebbels, once claimed that 'he who knows everything is afraid of nothing' (cited in Virilio 2009: 75). Given what we know about Goebbels and his regime, we have every reason to fear systems that want to know everything. Fighting for civil liberties, defending the right to privacy, challenging the coercive abuses of the myriad 'metrics' spawned by neo-corporate managerial practices represent an important re-affirmation of freedom, alongside justice and sustainability, as a core value of an operational politics of microspection.

If we conceive then of micro-modernity as the site of an infinitely extendable working out of what it is to be human and an articulation of the complexity of the non-human, does the very notion itself bring with it the danger of political impotence, social irrelevance, the scale a promise of marginalization not liberation? If capital operates globally and is perfectly comfortable with the master narratives of 'structural adjustment' and 'market disciplines' is there an element of self-delusion in looking to the primacy of the local, losing ourselves in fragmented pockets of detail? The first question to ask is whether the implicit assumptions of the questions are correct at a broader level. What is inherent in the critique of the political effectiveness of the local is a way of thinking about politics and culture which is beholden to an apparently self-evident duality, parts go up to make wholes. The local is a constituent part of a larger, global whole. But the question that might be asked about the linear reductionism of this part-whole paradigm is whether there are dominant metaphors or paradigms that obscure rather than clarify our thinking on political action among other things? John Urry notes that, 'In modern industrial societies, dominant metaphors were those of the clock, modern machinery (train, car, assembly line) and the photographic lens.' In contrast, he argues the 'hologram is a complex metaphor for a complex informational age. Information in a hologram is not located in any particular part of it. Rather any part contains, implies and resonates information of the whole' (Urry 2003: 50). In drawing our attention to the complexity of the part, this hologramatic vision concurs with the attention to the fractal intricacy of the particular that we have repeatedly stressed in this essay. What characterizes the transition initiatives that we mentioned earlier is that each initiative at local level contains within it an awareness of the global reasons and consequences of local actions. In this sense, a transition initiative is hologramatic by nature as it 'contains, implies and resonates information of the whole.'

'How Little Things Can Make a Big Difference' is the clearly visible sub-title of Malcolm Gladwell's *The Tipping Point* (2001). Gladwell's examples range from a small group of urban fashion-istas precipitating a dramatic change in the global sales of Hush Puppies to a startling reduction in crime statistics due to a determination to prosecute minor as well as major offences. What is implied is that small changes, micro-shifts, the actions of a relatively small number of individuals, can have significant effects. Placing the powerlessness of the local in contrast to the overwhelming force of the global may be to misunderstand the nature of change and the prevalence of what evolutionists call punctuated equilibrium in our society, namely, apparently sudden, radical shifts in the dominant state of affairs (Gould 1990: 2-3). An important notion which Gladwell borrows from the anthropologist Robin Dunbar is the idea of 'social channel capacity'. This is the ability we have to 'know' other members of a group, the limits on our information processing capacity in terms of getting to know people. In other words, each new encounter places extra strain on our existing capacity to manage the social and intellectual burden of establishing meaningful relationships with others. Dunbar argues that the optimal number of people it is possible for human beings to have a credible social interaction with over an extended period is around 150:

The figure of 150 seems to represent the maximum number of

individuals with whom we can have a genuinely social relationship, the kind of relationship that goes with knowing who they are and how they relate to us. Putting it another way, it's the number of people you would not feel embarrassed about joining uninvited for a drink if you happened to bump into them in the bar. (cited in Gladwell 2000: 179)

The significance of the concept of social channel capacity is that it points to the viability of concerted, knowledgeable political interaction happening not with greatly expanded but with greatly reduced numbers. The existence of distant links and weak ties of course greatly maximises the potential connectedness of any group but in the first instance it is what is manageable in terms of social interaction in the immediate environment that will contribute to effectiveness and sustainability of action for change. A politics of re-enchantment is not simply or only a matter of seeing the world anew, it is also about conceiving of the very ability to live differently. Often, this transformative promise can seem to be compromised by a question of scale. How is it possible to effect change in face of such overwhelming odds, in the light of the corporate takeover of the planet and its resources (Hertz 2002)? Implicit in Gladwell's case studies of change and Dunbar's observations on human capacity for social interaction, is that it is at local levels that political change is most not least effective and is more rather than less likely to ultimately precipitate significant change. To make democratic freedom a workable reality as opposed to an empty promise, it is the local, the particular and the specific, approached from the standpoint of a politics of microspection, which offer not only a vision of a planet that is infinitely expansive in its richness and difference but which allows the denizens of the planet to plot a course which does not result in the ultimate shrinkage of self-annihilation. Rediscovering the world is also about recovering the world and recovering the world is about recovering for present and future generations the lost values of sustainability, justice and freedom.

Endnotes

1 Dans l'univers littéraire, si l'espace des langues peut, lui aussi, être représenté selon une « figuration florale », c'est-à-dire un système où les langues de la périphérie sont reliées au centre par les polyglottes et les traducteurs, alors on pourra mesurer la littérarité (la puissance, le prestige, le volume de capital linguistico-littéraire) d'une langue, non pas au nombre d'écrivains ou de lecteurs dans cette langue, mais au nombre de polyglottes littéraires (ou protagonistes de l'espace littéraire, éditeurs, intermédiaires cosmopolites, découvreurs cultivés...) qui la pratiquent et au nombre de traducteurs littéraires – tant à l'exportation qu'à l'importation – qui font circuler les textes depuis ou vers cette langue littéraire.

2 Roinn siad saol is teanga, brón is áthas, gliondar is briseadh croí, sheas siad le chéile ag baisteadh is pósadh, thóg ualach a chéile idir chliabhán is chónra agus bí cinnte má bhain an saol tuisle asat ar an mbóthar go mbeadh lámh do chomharsan faoi do chloigeann sula mbuailfeá le talamh é.

3 Seo é an teach agam, seo iad mo mhuintir agus seo é mo shaol, a bhí mé ag ceapadh sular thit mo chodladh orm sa tolg agus mé ag brionglóidí ar a bheith in áit éigin eile ar thaobh eile an domhain seachas a bheith i m'aonar i gnarraí leathscoite i mo shaoránach i measc na saoránach leathscoite ag casadh na cré ar mhaithe lena casadh go dté mé lá éigin inti, cré dhubh mo mhéine, cré fhuar na cille. (142)

4 '...liquidation systématique des modalités d'existence de la figure de l'Autre.'

5 Si les différences peuvent proliférer, c'est parce que l'Autre n'est plus là pour leur faire barrage globalement : le concept métaphysique de l'Autre est ce qui contenait (au double sens d'englober et de retenir-empêcher-freiner) les différences,

puisqu'il représentait la différence absolue face à laquelle les différences et microdifférences qui coexistent aujourd'hui n'avaient pas le moindre sens en elles-mêmes. (63)

6   '...un esclave qui est maître en meme temps, tout en restant esclave, figure où maître et esclave sont littéralement indistincts, sans pour autant être confondus'

7   L'absence de temps, spécifique de la marche de la démocratie vers son accomplissement, fait que, pour être et avoir lieu, tout doit être et avoir lieu en même temps, c'est-à-dire dans le même espace.

8   La literature créole se moquera de l'Universel, c'est-à-dire de cet alignement déguisé aux valeurs occidentales[...]cette exploration de nos particularités[...]ramène au naturel du monde, [...]et oppose à l'universalité la chance du monde diffracté mais recomposé, l'harmonisation consciente des diversités préservées: la Diversalité.

9   Pour chaque bâtiment, les architectes sont amenés à se concentrer sur un lieu, à l'explorer, à essayer de connaître son histoire, comprendre ses forces, ses propriétés, les habitudes de ses habitants, la vie du quartier. Une contemplation active permet de mieux le saisir.

10 '...l'importance acordée aujourd'hui, par les enterprises, à l'EXTERNALISATION de leur production – y compris celle de la recherché et du développement de l'innovation – au detriment de leur ancienne localisation patrimoniale. Ainsi, depuis plusieurs années, l'*extérieur* l'emporte partout sur l'*intérieur*, et l'histoire géophysique se retourne, tel un gant!'

11 En 1977, j'écrivais que la vitesse est la vieillesse du monde. Trente ans plus tard, la preuve en est faite, puisque l'impact de la MOBILISATION GLOBALE vient frapper de plein fouet l'économie politique de la richesse des nations qui faisaient fi, jusque-là, de ce principe d'accélération qui allait pourtant remettre en cause l'histoire d'un progrès technique incompatible avec la réserve quantitative nécessaire à la

survie des nations.

12 '...le ciel l'emporte désormais sur le sol.'

13 '...chaque fois que s'accroît la rapidité du movement, le contrôle et sa traçabilité augmentent d'autant.'

14 Le véritable ami des libertés s'en tient à une conviction; mis à part les contes de fées où le faible devient fort (rêve révolutionnaire), pour les libertés effectives, il n'est en dernière instance qu'un seul garant matériel, nécessaire, même s'il n'est pas suffisant – le droit au secret, garanti au plus faible à l'égard du plus fort.

15 Sans doute en pleine conscience de ce qu'il faisait, il choisit de tout transformer en choses: la politique, les homes, l'histoire, Staline lui-même. Le règne absolu des choses, il l'appelait la mort ; il affirmait qu'à la fin, il n'y a qu'elle qui gagne.

References

Appadurai, A. (2006) *Fear of Small Numbers: An Essay on the Geography of Anger*, Durham NC: Duke University Press.

Augé, M. (1985) *La Traversée du Luxembourg*, Paris: Hachette.

Augé, M. (1986) *Un ethnologue dans le métro*, Paris: Hachette.

Baker, C. (2000) *A Parents' and Teachers' Guide to Bilingualism*, 2nd edition, Clevedon: Multilingual Matters.

Barabási, Albert-László (2003), *Linked: How Everything is Connected to Everything Else and What It Means for Business, Science, and Everyday Life*, New York: Plume.

Benasayag, M. and del Rey, A. (2007) *L'éloge du conflit*, Paris: La Découverte.

Bernabé, J., Chamoiseau, P. and Confiant, R. (1989) *Eloge de la créolité*, Paris: Gallimard.

Bischoff, A. and Loutan L. (2004) 'Interpreting in Swiss Hospitals'. *Interpreting*, 6 (2), 181-204.

Blommaert, J. (2005) 'Bourdieu the Ethnographer: The Ethnographic Grounding of Habitus and Voice'. *The Translator*, 11(2), 219-236.

Boland, R. (1992) *Sea Legs : hitch-hiking the coast of Ireland alone*, Dublin: New Island.

Bongie, C. (1991) *Exotic Memories: Literature, Colonialism and the Fin de Siècle*, Stanford, Calif.: Stanford University Press.

Bradley, Finbarr and Kennelly, James (2008) *Capitalising on Culture, Competing on Difference*, Dublin: Blackhall Publishing.

Brand, Stewart (2000) *The Clock of the Long Now: Time and Responsibility*, London: Phoenix..

Brook, T. (2008) *Vermeer's Hat: The 17th Century and the Dawn of the Global World*, London: Profile.

Brown, J.S. and Weiser, M. (1996) 'The Coming age of Calm Technology'. Available online: http://www.ubiq.com/hypertext/weiser/acmfuture2endnote.htm (accessed 1 March

2009).

Bouvier, N. (1990) *Journal d'Aran et d'autres lieux*, Paris : Payot.

Calvino, I. (1986) *Mr. Palomar*, tr. William Weaver, London: Picador.

Campbell, S. and Fainstein, S. (2003) *Readings in Planning Theory*, Oxford: Blackwell.

Casanova, P. (1999). *La République mondiale des lettres*, Paris : Seuil.

Clark, D.G. (2007) *A Farewell to Alms : A Brief Economic History of the World*, Princeton: Princeton University Press.

Clifford, J. (1992), 'Travelling Cultures', 96-111 in Grossberg, L., Nelson, C. and Treichler, P.A. (eds.) (1992) *Cultural Studies*, London: Routledge.

Convery, Frank (2007) 'Climate change must be factored into every aspect of our lives', *The Irish Times*, 7 April.

Crane, D. (2002) *Global Culture*, London and New York: Routledge.

Cronin, M. (2003) *Translation and Globalization*, London and New York: Routledge.

Cronin, M. (2008) 'Minding Ourselves: A new face for Irish Studies', *The Field Day Review*, 4, 175-185.

Cummins, J. (2000) *Language, power and pedagogy. Bilingual children in the crossfire*, Clevedon: Multlingual Matters.

Davies, N. and Moorhouse, R. (2002) *Microcosm: portrait of a Central European city*, London: Cape.

de Kerorguen, Y. (2009) 'L'économie sociale, une réponse au capitalisme financier?', *Le monde diplomatique*, 664, juillet, 8-9.

Delisle, J. and Woodsworth, J. (Eds.) (1995) *Translators through History*, Amsterdam: John Benjamins.

Dennis, K. and Urry, J. (2007) *The Digital Nexus of Post-Automobility*, Dept. of Sociology, Lancaster University.

De Maistre, X. (1959) *Voyage autour de ma chambre*, Paris : Laffont (originally published 1794).

De Zengotita, T. (2005) *Mediated: How the Media Shape Your World*, London: Bloomsbury.

Duhigg, C. (2009) 'Post-Meltdown, Traders Gain an Edge in Milliseconds', *The New York Times*, 1 August.

Dupin, E. (2009) 'La décroissance, une idée qui chemine sous la récession', *Le Monde Diplomatique*, 665, août, 20-21.

Edwards, J. (1995) *Multilingualism*, London: Penguin.

Elliott, E. and Lemert, C. (2006) *The New Individualism: the emotional costs of globalization*, London: Routledge.

Ennis, Séamus (2006) *Ceol, Scéalta, Amhráin*, Dublin: Gael-Linn.

Enright, Anne (2007) *The Gathering*, London: Jonathan Cape.

European Commission (2009) 'Social Economy'. Available online: http://ec.europa.eu/enterprise/entrepreneurship/craft/social_e conomy/soc-eco_intro_en.htm (accessed 10 August 2009).

European Commission against Racism and Intolerance (2007) *Third Report on the Netherlands*. Available online: http://hudoc.ecri.coe.int/XMLEcri/ENGLISH/Cycle_03/03_Cb C_eng/NLD-CbC-III-2008-3-ENG.pdf (accessed 12 March 2009).

Fitoussi, J-P and Éloi, L. (2008) *La nouvelle écologie politique : économie et développement humain*, Paris : Seuil.

Forsdick, C. (2005) *Travel in Twentieth-Century French and Francophone Cultures: The Persistence of Diversity*, Oxford: Oxford University Press.

Förster, M., Jesuit, D. and Smeeding, T. (2003) 'Regional Poverty and Income Inequality in Central and Eastern Europe: Evidence from the Luxembourg Income Study'. World Institute for Development Economics Research, Discussion Paper no. 2003/65. Available online: http://www.wider. unu.edu/publications/dps/dps2003/dp2003-065.pdf. (Accessed 11 December 2006).

Friedman, T. (2006) *The World is Flat: The Globalized World in the Twenty-First Century*, London: Penguin.

Fukuyama, F. (1992) *The End of History and the Last Man*, London: Hamish Hamilton.

Gaffney, M. (2007) 'What's the Craic?', *Irish Times Magazine*, 25

August.

Giddens, A. (1990) *The Consequences of Modernity*, Stanford, Calif.: Stanford University Press.

Gladwell, M. (2001) *The Tipping Point; How Little Things Can Make A Big Difference*, London: Abacus.

Gleick, J. (1987) *Chaos: Making a New Science*, London, Cardinal.

Gould, S.J. (1990) *Time's Arrow, Time's Cycle: Myth and Metaphor in the Discovery of Geological Time*, London: Penguin.

Granovetter, M.S. (1973) 'The Strength of Weak Ties', *The American Journal of Sociology*, 78, 1360-1380.

Greenfield, A. (2006) *Everyware: The dawning age of ubiquitous computing*, Berkeley, CA: New Riders.

Hall, S. (2002) 'Political Belonging in a World of Multiple Identities', 25-31, in Vertovec, S. and Cohen, R. (eds), *Conceiving Cosmopolitanism: theory, context, practice*, Oxford: Oxford University Press.

Heidegger, M. (1977) *The Question concerning Technology and Other Essays*. New York: Harper.

Heise, U.K. (2008) *Sense of Place and Sense of Planet: the environmental imagination of the global*, Oxford: Oxford University Press.

Hertz, N. (2002) *The Silent Takeover: Global Capitalism and the Death of Democracy*, London: Arrow.

Hopkins, R. & Lipman, P. (2009) *The Transition Network Ltd: Who We Are And What We Do*. Available online: http://www.transitionnetwork.org/Strategy/TransitionNetwork-WhoWe AreWhatWeDo.pdf (accessed 12 August 2009).

Illich, I. (1995) *Deschooling Society*, London: Marion Boyars (first published 1972).

Ingold, T. (2000) *The Perception of the Environment: Essays in Livelihood, Dwelling and Skill*, London and New York: Routledge.

Jacobs, J. (2000) *The Death and Life of Great American Cities*, London: Pimlico (originally published 1962).

Jonas, H. (1985) *The Imperative of Responsibility: In Search of an Ethics for the Technological Age*, tr. H. Jonas and Herr, D., Chicago: University of Chicago Press.

Julien, F. (2008) *De l'universel, de l'uniforme, du commun et du dialogue entre les cultures*, Paris : Fayard.

Kirkpatrick, E.M. (1983) *Chambers 20th Century Dictionary*, Edinburgh: W&R Chambers.

Klein, N. (2007) *The Shock Doctrine: The Rise of Disaster Capitalism*, London: Penguin.

Koren, L. (1994) *Wabi-Sabi for Artists, Designers, Poets and Philosophers*, Berkeley (Cal.): Stone Bridge Press.

Kundera, Milan (1996) *Slowness*, tr. Linda Asher, London: Faber and Faber.

Laval, C. (2007) *L'Homme économique : essai sur les racines du néolibéralisme*, Paris : Gallimard.

Lentin, A. (2004) 'The Problem of Culture and Human Rights in the Response to Racism', in Titley, G. (ed.) *Resituating Culture*, Strasbourg: Council of Europe, 95-103.

Mandelbrot, B. (1977) *The Fractal Geometry of Nature*, New York, Freeman.

Lyons, J. (2009) *The House of Wisdom: How the Arabs Transformed Western Civilization*, London: Bloomsbury.

Maspero, F. (1990) *Les Passagers du Roissy Express*, Paris : Seuil.

Maspero, F. (1994) *Roissy Express: A Journey through the Paris Suburbs*, tr. Paul Jones, London: Verso.

Massey, D. (2004) *For Space*. London: Sage.

McGee, H. and O'Brien, T. (2008) 'Ireland far off emissions and waste targets, says EPA report', *The Irish Times*, 9 October.

McIntosh, A. (2002) *Soil and Soul: People versus Corporate Power*, London: Aurum.

McIntosh, A. (2008) *Hell and High Water: Climate Change, Hope and the Human Condition*, Edinburgh: Birlinn.

McWilliams, D. (2005) *The Pope's Children: Ireland's New Elite*, Dublin: Gill and Macmillan.

McWilliams, D. (2008) *The Generation Game*, Dublin: Gill and Macmillan.

Millennium Ecosystem Assessment (2005) *Ecosystems and Human Well-Being: Synthesis*, Washington D.C.: Island Press.

Milner, Jean-Claude (2005) *La politique des choses*, Paris : Navarin.

Mitchell, W. (1995) *City of Bits: space, place and the Infobahn*, Cambridge, Mass.: MIT Press.

Montesquieu, C.-L. (1964) *Lettres Persanes*, Paris: Garnier-Flammarion (originally published 1724).

Montesquieu, C.-L. (2008) *Persian Letters*, tr. Andrew Kahn and Margaret Mauldon, Oxford : Oxford University Press.

Morin, E. (1999) *La tête bien faite*, Paris : Seuil.

Nolan, B. and Maître, B. (2007) 'Economic Growth and Income Inequality: Setting the Context', 27-42, in Fahey, Tony, Russell, Helen, Whelan, Christopher T. (eds.) *Best of Times: The Social Impact of the Celtic Tiger*, Dublin: IPA.

Novak, M. (2009) 'Transarchitecture'. Available online: http://framework.v2.nl/archive/archive/node/notion/.xslt/nod enr-127479 (accessed 30 May 2009).

O'Carroll-Kelly, R. (2008) *South Dublin: How to Get by on, Like, 10,000 Euro a Day*, Dublin: Penguin Ireland.

Ó Cróinín, D. (ed.) (2008) *A New History of Ireland: Prehistoric and Early Ireland*, Oxford: Oxford University Press.

Organisation for Economic Co-operation and Development (2007) *OECD Environmental Performance Reviews: China*. Available online: http://www.oecd.org/document/47/0,3343 ,en_2649_34307_37809647_1_1_1_1,00.html (accessed 25 August 2009).

Ong, W.J. (1989) *Orality and Literacy*, London and New York: Routledge.

O'Reilly, E. (2004) 'What has happened to us?', *The Irish Times*, 11 November.

Ó Treasaigh, L. (2007) *Cnoc na Lobhar*, Baile Átha Cliath: Cois Life.

Perec, G. (1974) *Espèces d'espaces*, Paris: Galilée.

Perec, G. (2008) *Species of Spaces and Other Pieces*, London : Penguin.

Perec, G. (1982) *Tentative d'épuisement d'un lieu parisien*, Paris : Bourgois.

Perec, G. (2010) *An Attempt at Exhausting a Place in Paris*, tr. Marc Lowenthal, Adelaide : Wakefield Press.

Perec, G. (1989) *L'infra-ordinaire*, Paris : Seuil.

Phipps, A. (2007) *Learning the Arts of Linguistic Survival: languaging, tourism, life*. Clevedon: Channel View.

Pratt, G. and Hanson, S. (1994) 'Geography and the Construction of Difference'. *Gender, Place, Culture*, 1(1), 5-29.

Pratt, M.L. (1992) *Imperial Eyes: Travel Writing and Transculturation*. London and New York: Routledge.

Prendergast, C. (2004) 'Introduction', in Prendergast, C. (ed.) *Debating World Literature*, London: Verso, vii-xiii.

Quessada, Dominique (2007) *Court traité d'altéricide*, Paris: Gallimard.

Rahman, Z.H. (2006) 'Hope of escape lost in translation', *The Sunday Times*, 17 December.

Ricardo, D. (2004) *The Principles of Political Economy and Taxation*, London: Dover (first published 1817).

Richards, T. (1993) *The Imperial Archive: Knowledge and the Fantasy of Empire*, London: Verso.

Robinson, Tim (1995) *Stones of Aran: Labyrinth*, Dublin: Lilliput Press.

Rorty, R. (1980) *Philosophy and the Mirror of Nature*, Oxford: Blackwell.

Simon, S. (2006) *Translating Montreal: Episodes in the Life of a Divided City*, Montreal and Kingston: McGill-Queens University Press.

Slater, E. (1998). 'Becoming an Irish *Flâneur*', Eamonn Slater and Michel Peillon (Eds.), *Encounters with Modern Ireland*. Dublin: Institute of Public Administration.

Seek, N.H. (2006) 'International Property Investment Trends'. Available online: http://www.prres.net/Papers/Seek_Inter national_Property_Investment_Trends.pdf. (accessed 5 December 2006).

Sassen, S. (1999) *Guests and Aliens*, New York: New Press.

Sassen, S. (2006) *Cities in a World Economy*, 3rd ed., London: Sage.

Sharpe, B. and Hodgson, T. (2006) *Towards a Cyber-Urban Ecology*, London: Foresight.

Sennett, R. (2002) 'Cosmopolitanism and the Social Experience of Cities'. In Vertovec, S. and Cohen, R. (Eds.), *Conceiving Cosmopolitanism: Theory, Context, Practice* (pp. 42-7). Oxford: Oxford University Press.

Sheller, M. (2003) *Consuming the Caribbean : from Arawaks to zombies*, London and New York: Routledge.

Simon, S. (2006) *Translating Montreal: Episodes in the Life of a Divided City*, Montreal and Kingston: McGill-Queen's University Press.

Skutnabb-Kangas, T. (2000) *Linguistic genocide in education – or worldwide diversity and human rights?* Mahwah, NJ: Lawrence Erlbaum.

Sriskandarajah, D. (2006). 'UK must look at that other group of migrants'. *The Financial Times*, 7 August.

Szerszynski, B. and Urry, J. (2006). 'Visuality, mobility and the cosmopolitan: inhabiting the world from afar'. *The British Journal of Sociology*, 57(1), 113-131.

Testot, L. (2009) 'La naissance d'une histoire-monde', *Sciences humaines*, 200, 7-8.

Theroux, P. (1984) *The Kingdom by the Sea*, London: Penguin.

Thrift, N., May, J. and May, J. (2001) (eds) *Timescape*, London: Routledge.

Tollefson, J. W. (1989). *Alien Winds : the re-education of America's Indochinese refugees*, New York : Praeger.

Thibault, P. (2009) 'Plaidoyer pour une architecture lente', *Ecologik*, 09, juillet-août, 114-115.

Tomlinson, J. (1999) *Globalization and Culture*, Chicago : Chicago University Press.

Trivedi, H. (2004) 'CyberCoolies: Call center workers are the new slave laborers of the 21st century', *Little India*, 5 October. Available online: http://www.littleindia.com/news/143/ ARTICLE/1507/2004-10-05.html (accessed 31 August 2007).

Tufte, E.R. (1990) *Envisioning Information*, Graphics Press: Cheshire (Conn.).

United Nations Population Division (2005). *International Migration and Development*, New York: United Nations.

Urbain, J. D. (1998) *Secrets de voyage: menteurs, imposteurs et autres voyageurs immédiats*, Paris : Payot.

Urry, J. (1990) *The Tourist Gaze: leisure and travel in contemporary societies*, London: Sage.

Urry, J. (2003) *Global Complexity* London: Sage.

Venturi, R. (1977) *Complexity and Contradiction in Architecture*. London: Architectural Press.

Virilio, P. (2009) *Le futurisme de l'instant : stop-eject*, Paris : Galilée.

Vitousek, P.M., Mooney, H.A., Lubchenco, J. and Melillo, J.M. (1997), 'Human domination of Earth's Ecosystems', *Science*, 277, 494-499.

Williams, R. (1979) *Politics and Letters*, London: New Left Books.

Wilson, E. (2002) *The Future of Life*, New York : Vintage Books.

About the Author

Michael Cronin is a critic, writer and broadcaster and lives in Dublin, Ireland. He holds a Personal Chair in the Faculty of Humanities and Social Sciences at Dublin City University. Among his single-author publcations are *Across the Lines: Travel, Language and Translation* (Cork University Press, 2000), *Translation and Globalization* (Routledge, 2003); *Time Tracks: Scenes from the Irish Everyday* (New Island 2003); *Translation and Identity* (Routledge, 2006) and he has co-edited *Reinventing Ireland: Culture, Society and the Global Economy* (Pluto Press, 2002), *Irish Tourism: Image, Culture, Identity* (Channel View, 2003) and *Transforming Ireland* (Manchester University Press, 2009). He is Humanities Secretary of the Royal Irish Academy.

zero
books

Contemporary culture has eliminated both the concept of the public and the figure of the intellectual. Former public spaces – both physical and cultural – are now either derelict or colonized by advertising. A cretinous anti-intellectualism presides, cheerled by expensively educated hacks in the pay of multinational corporations who reassure their bored readers that there is no need to rouse themselves from their interpassive stupor. The informal censorship internalized and propagated by the cultural workers of late capitalism generates a banal conformity that the propaganda chiefs of Stalinism could only ever have dreamt of imposing. Zer0 Books knows that another kind of discourse – intellectual without being academic, popular without being populist – is not only possible: it is already flourishing, in the regions beyond the striplit malls of so-called mass media and the neurotically bureaucratic halls of the academy. Zer0 is committed to the idea of publishing as a making public of the intellectual. It is convinced that in the unthinking, blandly consensual culture in which we live, critical and engaged theoretical reflection is more important than ever before.